BELIEVER'S RIGHTS & PRIVILEGES

Plus, Believer's Responsibilities

CYRIL O. URAMU

authorHOUSE®

AuthorHouse™
1663 Liberty Drive
Bloomington, IN 47403
www.authorhouse.com
Phone: 1 (800) 839-8640

Published by AuthorHouse 05/14/2018

ISBN: 978-1-5462-2186-9 (sc)
ISBN: 978-1-5462-2185-2 (e)

Print information available on the last page.

CONTENTS

INTRODUCTION

The inspiration to write this book came some 15 years ago in the beginning of my walk with the Lord. Though I have been a church member all along, but was not born again until then.

The initial title of this book was covenant blessings or promises. I had a leading to write about God's blessings for His children (believers), who are in covenant relationship with their Father. The Bible shows that believers are in covenant relationship with God (Ps 50:5).

Believers are the people who have made covenant with God by sacrifice. What sacrifice? The blood of Jesus Christ, shed at Calvary cross in atonement for the sins of the world (Matt 20:28).

By definition, a covenant is an agreement that fulfills, and demands a commitment. God commits to adopt and bless the man, who has committed to believe and accept Jesus Christ as Lord and Savior. It's commitment on the side of God because He promises and does not take back or lie about it (Num. 23:19). For a man, obedience is commitment; and obedience guarantees rewards of blessings. That's why I consider God's blessings on a believer as covenant blessings.

As it is customary to legal things, these blessings of God are signed in His Word (the Holy Bible), and effected by the instrumentality of the blood of Jesus Christ.

The blood of Jesus is the seal of the new covenant (Heb. 8:6). If Jesus had not gone to the cross, died and rose again, any claim of divine blessing will be in vain.

Jesus' death and resurrection is our guarantee. So, as a believer, you can claim any and every promise of God in His Word by faith, and it will work for you; because it's backed up by Christ's authority and standing in heaven (Col 2:14-15; Eph. 1:3-14, 20-22; 2:5-6).

As you have seen, the caption of this book is *Believer's Rights and Privileges*. Rights and privileges are on the same page (of relationship). By our faith in Christ, and our standing in Him, we have inheritance in God. We have right to the covenant promises in the Bible (His Word).

The second epistle of Peter in Chapter One says God by His divine power has given to us believers all things that pertain to life and godliness. These covenant blessings are in His Word. By His name *Jehovah Jireh*, God has made abundant provisions for every need of our lives, and these great provisions are contained in His Word (verse 3-4).

In this book, I have tried to x-ray a few of these covenant promises or blessings. Why many Christians live below God's best for their lives is ignorance or apathy to the Word of God. No wonder the Bible says, *my people are destroyed for lack of knowledge* (Hos. 4:6).

Study and chew this book, and discover the amazing provisions of divine treasures of blessings for you a believer. The Bible contains diverse promises for every situation of life. Study the Bible, know and claim these promises, and see how rich you are as a believer. Through His Word, God has spiritually provided for every need of your life (Eph. 1:3).

I pray, in reading this book, you will re-discover yourself in the pages of His Word. Shalom!

Cyril O. Uramu.

CHAPTER 1

Believer's Inheritance

One common theme in the Psalms is the reference to Israel as God's inheritance. This suggests that, there is something we can inherit from God. But, do believers really have rights and privileges accruable to them? Are there inheritances we can claim as believers?

In this book, our focus and searchlight is on spiritual inheritance, not on physical or material inheritance.

Jesus Christ told a parable (Luke 15:11-31) about a man who had two sons. The younger son came to his father, and demanded his inheritance –his share of his father's estate (Luke 15:11). The portion of goods or share of the estate that belonged to the boy is what we refer to here as physical or material inheritance.

Inheritance is a possession we receive as a right or by legal succession or bequest, after the owner's death. As we have physical inheritance so also we have spiritual inheritance.

Spiritual inheritance is the rights and privileges of believers; they are particular benefits, advantages or favor that believers enjoy or can claim and enjoy.

Spiritual inheritance can also be described as preferential treatment a believer in Christ receives; they are rights a believer claims by his association with Christ. The rights are legal or moral entitlement that accrues to us, being the beloved of God. The Bible confirms this in the First epistle of Peter.

1 Peter 1:3-5

> **3 Blessed be the God and Father of our Lord Jesus Christ, who according to His abundant mercy has begotten us again to a living hope through the resurrection of Jesus Christ from the dead,**
>
> **4 to an inheritance incorruptible and undefiled and that does not fade away, reserved in heaven for you,**
>
> **5 who are kept by the power of God through faith for salvation ready to be revealed in the last time.**

The above Scriptures are pointing to man's origin and fall, in contrast to his current standing. Adam (and all his descendants) were 'disenfranchised', as it were, when Adam disobeyed God, and sold out to Satan.

Before then, Adam had all things, being on the top of creation. He was created, greatly endowed and empowered by God (Ps. 8:4-6). But, when he committed sin, he lost, firstly his position (as the god of the earth), and secondly, his authority/inheritance.

And so, First Peter 1:3 says, through the death and resurrection of Jesus Christ, God *begotten us again,* first, to *a living hope,* and second, *to an inheritance.*

There are three significant points we need to take note of concerning First Peter 1:3.

1. We are *begotten again.* This means *born again –* a reference to *new birth.* Adam suffered spiritual death; and the same fate confronted his descendants after him. Spiritual death means separation from God in time and eternity. But through the death and resurrection of Jesus Christ, by our faith in Him, we became born again (new birth is given to us). Spiritual death was taken off our heads, so to speak; we were revived, having been dead in sins;

2. Restored *living hope –* Eph. 2:11-12 says anyone without Christ has no hope in the world. A man without Christ has a hopeless existence – hope is dead in him. But, if you are in Christ, a *living hope* is restored to you – hope of resurrection to eternal life; hope of seeing God, and hope of heavenly reward or blessings. It's also a hope of fulfilling divine destiny; of being what God created you to be. That's why it's a living hope.

3. *Born again to an inheritance –* Adam's fall disinherited him and his descendants after him. Adam had no inheritance to bequeath to his offspring. What he inherited from God, he sold out to Satan. Satan even boasted to Christ saying, *"All these possessions are transferred to me"* (Luke 4:6). But to every believer,

by his faith in Christ, is *restored an inheritance, that is incorruptible, unchangeable, undefiled, imperishable and unfading.* This inheritance is not only to be enjoyed in heaven. It has earthly portion or provision. There are rights, privileges, special benefits, favor and advantages believers will enjoy here on earth first, before being given the heavenly portion, at the fullness of time, when at rapture we receive final, ultimate salvation –the *salvation ready to be revealed in the last time* (verse 5). This earthly portion of our inheritance is the burden of this book.

God, clearly as can be attested to by His Word, has given believers an enviable inheritance.

The Bible describes the Word of God as the Word of grace. Through this Word that changes not, God does not only edify and build us up; He gives us (believers) rich inheritance (Acts 20:32). This inheritance is the covenant blessings that came to us through God's promise, first to Abraham and his seed (Gal 3:17). Apostle Paul described it as the promise based on faith in Jesus Christ given to us who are believers(Gal 3:22). Our reward for faith in God's Word, and in the Living Word (Jesus Christ), is this covenant promise of a glorious inheritance.

This covenant promise is legal, unchangeable and eternal, because it is guaranteed by the life and blood of Jesus Christ (that is, His death and resurrection), by which He dethroned Satan, powers and principalities (Col 2:14-15)

The Bible's reference to handwriting of requirements represents in part, the satanic manipulations or devices that would have denied us permanently, access to our lost inheritance. But thank God for Jesus Christ, who cancelled, blotted out and wiped away the offending handwriting and its demands; and disarmed, dethroned and defeated the principalities and powers.

Col 1:12

> **12 giving thanks to the Father who has qualified us to be partakers of the inheritance of the saints in the light.**

This is quite exciting. Hallelujah! God through Christ has qualified and made us fit to share the glorious portion, which is the inheritance (blessings He has promised and reserved for His saints). This He did when He delivered us from the control and dominion of darkness, and transferred us into the kingdom of His beloved Son, Jesus Christ.

Foundation of Believers Inheritance

As we said earlier, Adam was disinherited when he committed treason, and sold his right to Satan. And so were all his descendants after him.

But, the God we serve is the God of restoration. For He has promised in Joel 2:25 that He will restore all our losses – the benefits and blessings Satan has stolen from us, and as well our lost seasons and glory.

Thank God for Jesus Christ, our chief corner stone and sure foundation. He is the Author, and the seal of our inheritance. By the counsel of God's will, He has pre-destined us to receive an inheritance, as the Bible says.

In Christ, believers have obtained a sweet inheritance, which was granted to us before the foundation of the world that we may be for glory of God for which we are re-created (Eph. 1:11-12).

Having believed in Christ, each Christian is sealed with the Holy Spirit of promise. The Holy Spirit Himself is the executor (and as well, *guarantor*) of our inheritance (that is, God's promises to believers); hence He is called the Holy Spirit of promise (Eph. 1:13-14). This means that, the indwelling presence of Holy Spirit through the new birth, is divine proof and confirmation, and assurance of our access to the promised blessings of God, which we have tagged believers rights and privileges. Apostle Paul described these as the riches of the glory of God's inheritance for us who believe (Eph. 1:18). Believers sure do have inheritance in God.

Jesus Christ is, no doubt, the source, the author, '*perfecter*' and finisher of our inheritance.

Col 3:24

> **24 knowing that from the Lord you will receive the reward of the inheritance; for you serve the Lord Christ.**

As the Mediator of the new covenant, Jesus Christ, by our faith in Him, delivers and guarantees not just our eternal inheritance, but also our blessings in the body of Christ (Heb. 9:15).

To cap it all, Paul's epistle to the Romans in chapter eight says,

Rom. 8:14, 17

> **14 For as many as are led by the Spirit of God, these are sons of God...**
>
> **17 and if children, then heirs — heirs of God and joint heirs with Christ, if indeed we suffer with Him, that we may also be glorified together.**

Believers by indwelling presence of the Holy Spirit, from the new birth, are led by the Holy Spirit, and hence are children of God. The Bible says we are not only children of God, but also heirs of God, and joint heirs with Christ. This proves beyond all doubts, that believers have rich inheritance in Christ of God.

Arising from this, the Bible declares in Cor. 3:31-32 that all things are yours, as a believer.

In the following chapters, we shall be discussing and answering the questions: who is a believer? What are the believer's rights and privileges?

CHAPTER 2

Who is a Believer?

To answer this question, some may point to where believers are found, the church. The church is the body of Christ to which Christ is the head (Eph. 1:22-23).

Bible scholars described the church as the assembly of the called out people: the people who are delivered out of the kingdom of darkness, the world (Col. 1:13). If what the Bible says is true (and I believe it is), Satan is the god of this world (John 14:30; 2 Cor. 4:4). But, Jesus is the Light of the world (John 8:12; 9:4).

Satan is the epitome of darkness, and the veritable ruler of darkness. Satan being the god of the world makes the world the dark kingdom by extension. Believers are surely in the world, but not under Satan's ruler-ship and control, because they have been translated into the kingdom of light (Col. 1:13). This, by the abundant grace of Christ is what makes believers the light of the world, and the salt of the earth (Matt. 5:13, 14).

For lack of better appellation, the church might be likened to a temporary "home" of believers. Of course, heaven is the eternal home of all believers, who are so-journeying on the earth (Phil 3:20; 1 Pet. 2:11). As Jesus had said, believers are in the world but they do not belong to the world (John 15:18).

There are two common terms that have been used interchangeably: Christian and believer. Is there any difference between them?

First, according to the accounts of the Acts of the Apostles, the Disciples of Christ were first called Christians in Antioch (Acts 11:26).

It goes without saying, therefore, that a disciple is a Christian, and a Christian is a disciple. But, who is a disciple? The early Bible characters called disciples were followers and friends of Jesus Christ (Matt. 10:1).

The early followers of Jesus Christ were not just His disciples, they were also His friends, and He called them so (John 15:13-15).

So, disciples are friends and followers of Jesus Christ, who were called and chosen by Him to learn of Him, and help His ministry. They were those who loved Jesus, who believed in Him, and kept His commandment. (John 14:21

It's important to note that, one of the qualifications for a disciple is that, he believes in the Master, and the work and the mission of the Master. If you believe on the Master and the mission of the Master, then indeed you are a disciple. If you don't believe, then you are not a disciple (that is, you are not a follower of the cause and the proponent of the cause).

Even from the beginning in His ministry, Jesus knew those who did not believe in Him, and who would betray Him (John 6:64-67).

So those who did not believe Him (Jesus) departed from Him, and ceased to be His disciples. A disciple believes and follows, because he believes the cause or the mission; and believes too in the proponent of the cause.

Thus, in modern times, a disciple is a follower of the followers of Christ, who themselves were believers in Christ, and followers of Christ. The Christian faith came to the Gentiles through Christ's disciples like Paul, who in epistles enjoined the Gentile Christians to pattern their lives after him as himself imitates Christ (1 Cor. 11:1).

You cannot follow what or whom you don't believe in. Amos 3:3 says, two cannot walk together except they are in agreement. This is to say, believing is an integral part of followership (discipleship). Followers of Jesus Christ are disciples of Christ. Just as followers are disciples, so believers are followers.

If the first disciples were called Christians, it follows, therefore, that Christians are believers (followers of Jesus Christ). A believer is a Christian, and a Christian is a believer.

Qualifications of a Believer

Now, we have said that the church is the gathering of the called out people. Can everyone who is in the church or attends a church be called a believer or a Christian? Is every church member a believer? Not necessarily.

There are qualifications for a believer (Christian). The Bible has made it expressly clear who believers are.

A Believer is One Who Believes

A believer is one who believes – who believes in Jesus Christ as the Messiah, the Savior and the Redeemer of the world. This, I suppose, is the primary qualification for a believer (a Christian). To believe Jesus as the Messiah is to believe in God.

Humanity was estranged and separated from God by the sin of Adam and Eve. But, God in Gen 3: 15 prophesied a time of restoration. Jesus Christ was sent by God at the fullness of time, to restore and return man to God, and to fellowship with God.

Adam was a son of God before he derailed, and became as a consequence, slave of Satan (Rom. 6:16). God sending Jesus Christ into the world was an act of mercy and love, to reclaim His sons and daughters stolen, as it were, by Satan.

John 1:12

> **12 But as many as received Him, to them He gave the right to become children of God, to those who believe in His name:**

Those whom God claims as His sons, and those who claim God as their Father, are those who believe in Jesus Christ.

The right of son-ship is given only to *those who believe in His name.*

The implication of John 1:12, is that, *even though God created everyone on the earth, not all are children of God.* If you don't believe in Jesus Christ, you are not a child of God (and you cannot claim to be a Christian or a believer).

There are children of God, and there are children of the devil (1 John 3:10). Rom. 6:16 says to whom you gave yourself up to obey (or believe in), that person is your master, and you are that person's servant. The day Adam listened to Satan and obeyed Satan, he ceased to be a son of God.

Believing in Jesus Christ is a key to receiving salvation – deliverance from death and hell. Jesus Christ is the Author of salvation for mankind. The Bible says expressly there is no other name given by God on earth by which men must be saved. It's only the name of Jesus Christ *(Acts 4:12).*

Concerning salvation, we must not only believe in Jesus, we must as well confess the Lordship of Jesus (Rom 10:9-10).

The Scriptures say specifically, as we believe with our hearts, we must also confess with our mouths to receive salvation. Therefore, a believer is one who believes Jesus Christ is the Son of God, who died on the cross for his sins, and was raised for his justification; and confesses Jesus as Lord and Savior.

A Believer is One Who is Regenerated

Regeneration is yet another key qualification for a believer. Unfortunately, regeneration is misunderstood by many so-called Christians.

Regeneration means to make anew something that is weak or dead. It's a recreation process; it refers to new birth.

Many Christians claim to be regenerated (that is, born again), yet they have little understanding of this concept and how it is achieved.

What does the Bible say about regeneration? Jesus Himself said pointedly to Nicodemus, unless a man be born again he cannot enter the heaven. Being born again is another word for regeneration. New birth or regeneration is a key requirement for a believer to make heaven (John 3:3-7).

Jesus made it categorically clear, except a man is born again (that is, regenerated), he cannot enter the kingdom of heaven. And He emphatically says a man must be born again (verse 7).

A believer is one who is born again. Being born again (regenerated) is a spiritual rather than a physical process. The two are separate but similar processes.

Jesus said, he who is born of the flesh (physical) is flesh, but he who is born of the Spirit (regeneration) is spirit (verse 6). Regeneration is a spiritual process because it's organized, performed and executed by the agency of the Holy Spirit.

A man, descended from Adam, carries with him Adam's perverted nature, clothed in unrighteousness. Because like Adam, he is subject to Satan, and is a slave of Satan – unclean and unholy.

In the process of being born again (salvation), the unclean and unholy vessel is recreated to bear the holy and perfect nature of holy God – the nature of righteousness. Thus, the Bible calls believers new creatures in Christ, because they are adorned with Christ's garment of righteousness, by the grace of God. Now, the sinful nature of Satan is done away with in them because they are regenerated, and delivered from spiritual death, and raised to a new life in Christ (2 Cor. 5:17).

The regeneration came about when, by the riches of God's mercy and grace, Jesus Christ took our sins on His own body on the cross, and died in our place that we may receive God's gift of righteousness (2 Cor. 5:21). It's a divine exchange that clothed us with the garments of salvation and covered us with the robe of righteousness (Isa. 61:10).

Being born again is to be born of the Spirit of God. Thus, the Bible refers to believers as being *born of God* (1 John 3:9; 5:1). Believers are those who are born of God.

How do we get born again or become regenerated? Many so-called Christians will tell you, they believe they are born again because they are water-baptized.

Water baptism is vital requirement for a believer because it's commanded by Christ (Mark 16:15-16; Matt 28:18-19). Regeneration is not water baptism but leads to it. Baptism does not make you born again or saved. It's because, you don't baptize unbelievers. You water baptize only believers.

As Jesus commanded in Mark 16:16, it's only those who believe who are to be baptized. This implies that one has to believe first before being baptized. So you are not born again (saved) because you are baptized.

Apostle Peter said we are born again through the incorruptible Word of God.

1 Peter 1:23

23 having been born again, not of corruptible seed but incorruptible, through the word of God which lives and abides forever,

A man becomes born again when he hears the Word of God, and believes with his heart that Jesus died for his sins, and he accepts and confesses with his mouth the Lordship of Christ (Rom.10:9-10). It's the Holy Spirit, through the Word, that generates the spiritual experience of new birth in a man (who is dead in sins and trespasses), turning him into a new creation in Christ Jesus. Then after being born again, you must of course be water baptized as Christ commanded.

Being born again is a spiritual process, which draws you into a covenant relationship with Christ. Because, by the grace and mercy of God, you have become the righteousness of God in Christ, to love and honor God, and be rewarded with the inheritance of the saints in the light (Eph. 1:18;

Col. 1:12). What a wonder! What a glorious heritage the believer possesses!

A Believer is One Who has Eternal Life

Are you a believer? Do you have eternal life in you? I am at pain to observe that, there is monumental ignorance among Christians, over this subject, and regarding our overall standing in Christ. It's disquieting because we are in the end time, and believers ought to know and be sure of such matter.

But, one of the many qualifications for a believer is one who has eternal life. What does the Bible say regarding eternal life?

First, I am reminded of what Jesus told Martha in the gospel of John chapter eleven (verses 21-26).

In that discussion between Jesus and Martha, Jesus made a very important revealing declaration (though confusing to some). He said whoever lives and believes in Him shall never die.

Some have argued, "we are mere mortals, how is it that we shall never die?' Of course, you may not see the revelation He communicated right there except with spiritual eyes (Eph. 1:18).

In the above Scripture, Jesus was referring to eternal life. He who believes has this secret endowment called eternal life. It's the right of believers. Eternal life is the life of God in the believer (imparted by the Holy Spirit). That's why a believer does not die; the life of God cannot perish.

A believer undergoes a transitional departure (which the world calls death for themselves), to move from the earth to heaven (his ultimate home). That's why Paul cautioned the Thessalonians not to mourn (in the manner of the unbelievers) after those who sleep in the Lord. Believers don't die – they just sleep when it's time to go home. Hallelujah!

Let's explore other Scriptures on eternal life.

John 3:16

> **16 For God so loved the world that He gave His only begotten Son, that whoever believes in Him should not perish but have everlasting life.**

The same claim is yet repeated above. He who believes in Christ has eternal life (or everlasting life). The writer of the first epistle of John stated emphatically that God has given believers eternal life. And it's only those who believe in Christ that have this unique divine life (1 John 5:11-13).

This means that eternal life is not in every man upon the surface of the earth. It's only in the believers that everlasting life dwells. And the Bible warns apocalyptically in John gospel that unbelievers do not have eternal life, but rather faces the rod of wrath (John 3:35-36).

Unbelievers will abide in, and suffer the wrath of God. Great warning!

How do we receive eternal life? It's through the Holy Spirit, and by the Holy Spirit. It comes just by believing in Christ. The very moment you believe (and are saved), the Holy Spirit transfuses, invests, confers or imparts this life of God on the believer,(sincerely, I don't know exactly how). I can't tell how, but I believe the Holy Spirit does, and He does it perfectly and effortlessly, to the glory of God. So the Bible says, and I believe it.

A popular Nigerian Pentecostal Bishop is given to saying *"I am un-killable"* What is his boast? What is his confidence? It's God's investment in his life – the eternal life. The life of God cannot perish. If you are a genuine believer, know it too, that you are *un-killable*, by the same token. Hallelujah!

Of course, as believers, we can only boast of what the Lord is doing or has done in our lives.

A Believer is One Who is the Salt and the Light

Jesus Himself is the light of the world (John 8:12)

This present world is in darkness because of pervasive wickedness and evil; and the ruler of this dark world is Satan. And all the unbelievers of this world are subject to Satan, the chief darkness.

Christ is the light of the world. Believers are not subject to Satan but to Christ. According to the above Scripture, believers, as followers of Christ have the light of life, courtesy of Christ, and by the mercy and grace of God. The gospel of John 1:4 says that in Christ was life, and that life was the light of all men.

Therefore, a believer cannot walk in darkness (except he chooses to, or by consent of ignorance, or in error). Christ said pointedly that believers are the salt of the earth and the light of the world (Matt 5:13-14).

Yes indeed, believers are the light of the world, and the salt of the earth. That means that, believers are to point the world (unbelievers) to Christ, to righteousness; to godly conduct and holy living.

Believers are to be examples to the world in word, in love, in truth, in purity, in faith, in conduct, in spirit and in worship. This is how they can be the light of the world that is in darkness, and the salt of the earth that is overwhelmed by bitterness of sin and perversion, and ungodly living/associations.

In contrast, the Bible calls unbelievers darkness (Eph. 5:8 says). Every unbeliever belongs to the kingdom of darkness, whose chief ruler is Satan.

But believers are light, who belong to the kingdom of light (the kingdom of God). So the Scripture calls believers children of light (Eph. 5:1-2).

Believers as light, are to imitate God (the Father of light), by walking in love; and as children of light show-casing their light and lightening the dark ways of the world - the evil world ruled by chief of darkness, Satan.

God is love (1 John 4:8); His nature is love. Like father like son. Believers are to walk in love, the glorious nature of their Father God, which they also have being children of God. As the Bible declares, the love of God has been shed in our hearts by the Holy Spirit (Rom 5:5). And this love makes us to hate sin and embrace righteousness (Ps. 97:10-12).

A Believer is one who is Called and Sanctified.

In Jer. 1:5, God says to Jeremiah, before I formed you in the womb, I knew you; I called you and sanctified you.

What God says to Jeremiah is also true of every believer. Every believer is called and sanctified (set apart for God's use).

Paul had prayed for the Ephesians that, the eyes of their understanding be enlightened (opened) to know the hope of God's calling for their lives.

There is no believer that is an accident of creation – that is, without divine purpose and assignment. Every believer has one calling or the other. That's what the Lord says in Rom. 11:29.

29 For the gifts and the calling of God are irrevocable.

And because a believer is called, he has at least one talent (gift) attached (or rather planted or buried) into his life or constitution. And to this talent is attached, accompanying sufficient grace to deliver the required result (Eph. 4:7).

This reminds me of parable of the talents (Matt. 25:14-30). There is no one believer without a gift. And God values this gift so much; hence the judgment of the one who buried his talent appeared extraordinarily hard. The master called him, lazy, slothful, wicked and unprofitable; he failed God's expectation, and the investment wrought upon his life.

And because of the vital position of a believer, with so much divine investment upon his life, God sanctifies him (setting him uniquely apart) to ensure his success, and heaven's expected dividend (Acts 20:32).

A Believer is one who is Holy

From the very beginning, we posted that, believers are children of God. According to the popular Bible saying, two individuals cannot walk together except they are in agreement (Amos 3:3).

Because believers are the *sons of God through faith in Christ Jesus* (Gal. 3:26); they are holy because they have a calling to live holy (1 Thess. 4:7).

Yes, believers have a calling to holiness. As believers, we are holy by the mercy and grace of God, who makes us righteous by our faith in Christ. Righteousness is God's gift to every believer (Rom 5:17).

God Himself calls the believer, elect, holy and beloved (Col. 3:12).

And believers are commanded to put on the bond of perfection, which is love. God is love, and love is the very nature of God (1 John 4:8). Believers who are recreated by the Holy Spirit share this holy love nature of God.

The Bible says God has shed His love upon our hearts, through the Holy Spirit (Rom. 5:5). Therefore, walking in this God-kind of love is a hallmark, and evidence of our salvation.

1 Peter 2:9

> **9 But you are a chosen generation, a royal priesthood, a holy nation, His own special people, that you may proclaim the praises of Him who called you out of darkness into His marvelous light;**

Who else could that be? **A holy nation, God's own special people, a chosen generation?** It's the generation of believers, of course. A believer is chosen and called not only to a divine assignment, but he is also called to holiness and obedience, and faithfulness.

If any calls himself a believer, and he is deliberately living in sin of any form or kind, he is self-deluded. He has lost his appointment and commission.

If you say you are a believer, you must remain pure just as He (Christ) is pure (1 John 3:3).

Other Names by which a Believer is known

Besides what we have already seen in the foregoing sections, there are other names by which a believer is known.

A believer, because he bears the Holy Spirit, he is called *the temple of God* (2 Cor. 6:16; 1 Cor. 3:16-17; 6:19-20). This appellation is derived from the indwelling presence of the Holy Spirit in the believer.

The Bible also calls believers *Christ* (2 Cor. 6:15), and *saints* (Acts 9:13; Rom. 1:7; 1 Cor. 1:2).

A believer is all of the above we say he is, but there are references in the Bible which are not for believers in Christ. Examples are **sons of disobedience** (Eph. 2:2; 5:6); **dogs** (Matt. 15:26-27; Phil 3:2; Rev 22:15); **lawlessness and belial** (2 Cor. 6:14, 15); **fornicator, unclean, covetous, idolater** (Eph. 5:5). No works of darkness are attached to a believer (Gal. 5:19-21; Eph. 5:11). These are references to unbelievers.

The foregoing, I believe has given enough contending grounds to know who a believer is; to whom the inheritance of the saints pertains. From these you will be able to judge if indeed you are a believer.

Every church member is not a believer. Even some who claim to be are not. The qualifications enumerated above tell, indeed, to whom the divine rights and privileges of the kingdom of God belong.

Nonetheless, there are some assemblies or 'church' groups who do not consider or call themselves believers or Christians.

Believers are those who believe in Christ; who are followers of Christ (Christians). So if anyone will exclude self or pays allegiance to another man in place of Christ, then that one, am afraid, is not a believer nor a Christian.

There are no two Jesus Christ – there is only one Jesus Christ, who had ascended into heaven (though He is omnipresent). Unfortunately, a lot of folks are being deceived and hoodwinked to claim and believe men living now among us (or recently dead) as Jesus Christ.

Don't be surprised about this. For the Bible had already warned about it (Matt 24:4, 23-24; 1 Tim 4:1-2).

I believe in the One and only One Jesus Christ of God, the Lord, Savior and Redeemer of my life. By His great grace and mercy, I am a believer and a recipient of the inheritance of the saints in the light.

Our position and standing as believers, I describe as wonderful wonder. We were all slaves of Satan having been sold to him by Adam. When God through the eternal blood of His Son, paid the price for our freedom, we became free from Satan's bondage. But, instead of us being just slaves or servants of God, God by the exceeding riches of His grace, adopted us as His children (Rom 8:15-16; Gal. 3:26; 4:5-6). So a believer is a child of God, not a slave or a servant. What a great privilege! What a great grace!

In the subsequent chapters, we shall be discussing some (not all) of the rights and privileges of believers. The foregoing I believe has been a good foundation and introduction to this all-important subject.

CHAPTER 3

Health and Long Life

One of the foremost rights of a believer is divine health and long life. Divine health is a state of perfect health; life without sickness or disease. Sickness or disease was not part of God's original design and plan for Adam and his descendants.

When Adam was created, there was not an iota of weakness or infirmity in him. The testimony of the Bible is that, everything God created (including Adam) was good. (Gen 1:31). Good means perfect without defects, without blemish, without weakness.

Sickness is a child of its mother sin, and father Satan. Sin is the main cause of sickness or disease. And death comes from diseases. Satan is the author, manufacturer and distributor of sin. The Bible calls sin the *works of Satan (1 John 3:8); unfruitful works of darkness (Eph. 5:11; Gal. 5:19-20).*

Adam was created with divine health – not to be sick, not to die. Sickness and death came into the world as a result of sin (Rom. 5:12).

But quite early in His dealings with children of Israel, His servant, God made it absolutely clear He will not permit them to be afflicted with diseases. He made it known that divine health was His design and plan for them. But to enjoy this, they were to fulfill a condition, which is, to listen carefully to His voice; do what is right, and obey His commands and decrees (Exod. 15:26).

God revealed Himself to Israel as the *Lord who heals them.* This was a solid, unbreakable, unbeatable assurance from God. They would enjoy divine health, if and only if, they would obey Him. This was to be a covenant blessing unto them – a reward of their obedience and love of their God and Maker.

Personally, I define covenant as an agreement that demands and fulfills a commitment. God commits to bless them with divine health as they commit to obey Him completely.

Note that in Deuteronomy 7:12-15 God promised to take away all forms of sickness from them. Not even the least of diseases was permitted to attach itself on them.

That text was a reminder to Israel of God's repeated promises of divine health, first in Exodus 15:26, and later in Exodus 23:25-26.

The covenant of divine health contained in the Word of God is one of the precious promises of God to His beloved people.

God had worked out a perfect plan to keep the children of Jacob in sound health and strength. Throughout their journey in the wilderness they enjoyed this great provision, and the Psalmist speaks of this in colorful words

Ps. 105:37

37 He also brought them out with silver and gold, and there was none feeble among His tribes.

None was ever sick among the congregation, as they journeyed toward the Promised Land. As the Scriptures say, God brought them out with great joy, to inherit the land and the labor of other nations (Ps. 105:42-45).

Yes, there was no feeble one (that is, sick) among them; they had joy and gladness. Joy and gladness are terms associated with a healthy man. Sickness brings grief and sorrow.

Even in the wilderness when they derailed by speaking against God and Moses, and God permitted them to be afflicted by serpentine bite, He readily and quickly worked out a plan for their healing, when they repented (Num. 20:4-9).

Talking further about this wonderful plan of God for His servants, the children of Jacob, the Psalmist says, God saved them out of all their distresses, delivering them from every sickness and hazard on the way (Ps. 107:19-20).

New Covenant, Better Promises

We have said so much about children of Israel, who were servants of God. What about the believers, who are the sons of God? The Bible confirms that believers have a better covenant through Jesus Christ (Heb. 7:22; 8:6).

Divine health is the birthright of believers, and it is anchored on the new covenant, which was guaranteed by the blood of Jesus Christ. Some 500 years before the birth of Jesus, Isaiah prophesied of the arrival of this new covenant.

Isaiah, 500 years earlier, prophesied that the Suffering Servant, who was to come, would bear our grief and sorrows; and for our total peace He would suffer afflictions (Isa. 53:4-5).

Who is this, who was to bear our *griefs* and *sorrows?* Who is He, who was to be afflicted for our peace? (This includes the peace of the body, which is healing). Who is He, whose stripes were to bring healing to the children of Jacob? It's Jesus Christ – the Savior of the world (Acts 8:26-35). Jesus is the personality to whom Isaiah's prophesy referred – the One who procured salvation, deliverance and healing for the children of Jacob.

Matthew the evangelist confirmed this in the gospel.

Matt. 8:17

> **17 that it might be fulfilled which was spoken by Isaiah the prophet, saying: "He Himself took our infirmities and bore our sicknesses."**

Jesus did not only work out our salvation when He went to the cross, He also carried our infirmities and bore our sicknesses. Isaiah's was a prophecy; Matthew's is a testimony of its fulfillment. That's why Jesus went about doing good, casting out demons and healing multitudes of diverse afflictions (Acts 10:38).

Jesus also gave His disciples the power to heal (Luke 9:1; Matt. 10: 1); and power over the devil and demons (Luke 10:19). You cannot give or share what you don't have. The disciples through Christ received divine health, and then were empowered to heal the sick (Mk. 16:16-18).

Divine healing is the right of believers. In His dialogue with a woman of Canaan, Jesus said to her, that it is not right to take the children's bread and cast it to the dogs (Matt. 15:26).

The term *dogs* refer to unbelievers, while *children* refer to believers. Jesus confirmed in that Scripture that healing is the right of children of God (believers). God does not get glory from our sickness or weakness. Infirmity cannot be His delight and design for His children. Our healing is His will and delight.

In fact, the Bible says in Ps 35:27 that God has interest in the prosperity of His servants.

Yes, God has pleasure in our prosperity (which includes sound health), not in our poverty or sickness.

Some years ago, I read a testimony of a Pastor. He was driving on a highway when suddenly he felt a sharp pain on the left side of the chest. And Satan whispered to his ear, 'heart attack; yes your two other brothers have had heart attack previously.'

He said to Satan, 'you are a liar, I don't have heart attack, and can't have heart attack.' He quickly packed his car on the side curb, got down from the car, and jogged on the side walk to over 1 km distance and back. Got into his car and drove off. That was the end of the story of heart attack.

That account was the beginning of my own testimony – my journey to divine healing. I had reasoned to myself, if God could do that for the Pastor, He could also do it for me. At that time I was having unrelenting fever for over two weeks. But after reading the testimony of the Pastor I discarded all the medicines I was given. And for the past sixteen years God has kept me in divine health.

Healing is the birthright of believers – the children's bread. A believer in Christ is not supposed to be sick. But many are, due largely to ignorance. Some claim that, sickness is a cross a Christian is supposed to carry. This is nothing but gross ignorance.

Sickness is not and cannot be a cross for a believer to carry. The Bible teaches that sickness is a curse of the law (Deut. 28:15-63; Gal 3:13). Jesus has already delivered believers from every curse of the law (which includes sickness).

Why will Jesus give us sickness as a cross to carry; sickness from which He has already saved us? Does that make any sense? Did He not go to the cross to save us and heal us?

Bible scholars say, the word salvation implies deliverance, preservation, safety, healing and soundness (from the Hebrew and Greek root words).

So, we were delivered from the curses of the law (sickness, poverty and eternal death) by the blood of Jesus Christ, on the account of our faith in Him. I reject the so-called cross of sickness; I claim divine health as my rightful inheritance, as a believer.

I sincerely sympathize with many in the body of Christ who are battling with various health conditions. If you don't know your inheritance, you cannot claim it, neither will you enjoy it. But if you know your rights, (and the inheritance which is legally yours), then you can make claims and succeed. The Bible says clearly that, divine health is believers' inheritance in Christ. Don't allow Satan cheat you out of what is your right.

Some years ago, I read a story of a 65-year old man, who was living in abject poverty – rummaging through refuse to eke out a living. But he did not know that an uncle before his death, had bequeathed to him one million dollars (then he was just four years old).

This man suffered all through his life, feeling abandoned and cheated by life. But the day he discovered his inheritance was the day the table turned for him. He made his claims, and got his rights. Many believers are just like this man – not knowing their inheritance in Christ, they struggle through life grappling with diverse diseases and afflictions.

In Acts 17: 25, it's written that God gives to all men life, breath, and all things to enjoy. Do you emerge all things will exclude good health?

Besides, James 1:17 says God gives us good and perfect gifts. What would you call good and perfect gift? Is it good health or sickness?

Sickness is evil, and Satan (the doer of evil) is the author of sickness. The good gift of God to us His children is divine health with wealth and joy.

Moreover, verse 28 of Acts 17 says it's in God we live, move and have our being. Sickness is darkness. Believers live and move in the Light (God). Light prevails over darkness (John1:5). Know your rights in Christ, believer. Stand in faith, and stop darkness (sickness and diseases) from infiltrating into your life.

Divine healing and health is God's perfect gift to you, believer. That's why God puts His Spirit in you at new birth, when you were recreated – born again (John 4:14; 2 Cor. 5:17). One of the principal works of the indwelling Holy Spirit is to re-vitalize and heal your mortal body (Rom 8:11).

To give life to your mortal body is to quicken or re-vitalize your body; that is the work of the Holy Spirit who dwells in you.

Any major disease destroys the cellular components of the body; snuffing life out of the cells, *railroading* the body to death. Diseases lead to death. As a believer, the Spirit of Christ dwelling in you gives life (and not death) to your body. The Spirit quickens your mortal body to divine health. That's your right as a believer.

Believer's Healing - a Settled Matter

Divine health is a believer's right. When Apostle Peter wrote to believers in the first epistle, he told them that their healing (or divine health) is a settled matter, not subject to any negotiation. He spoke of it as a matter of fact (or of divine truth, so to speak). He said to them, you were healed; (not, are to be healed; not, will be healed). But you WERE HEALED. When Jesus died on the cross and rose again, He made the needed provision (1 Peter 2:24).

To us living now, we can say we were healed over 2,000 years ago. When Christ died and rose again, our salvation as well as healing was executed and completed right then. There's nothing remaining to be done for a believer to enjoy divine health. I feel it's a matter of choice – you can chose to enjoy the inheritance of divine health which Christ has perfected for you 2,000 years ago or chose to carry 'evil cross' of sicknesses.

God delights, and takes glory from your being healthy and strong (3 John2).

Are you a Christian? It's your right not to be sick. It's your inheritance to enjoy divine health. Our God is *Jehovah Rapha – the Lord who heals.*

Long Life – Believer's Portion

Exodus 20:12 says, honor your parents that your days may be long. All the Patriarchs who lived before the law lived long lives. Exodus 20:12 shows that it's God's design that His people enjoy long life; untimely or premature death was not God's plan for His people.

In Exodus 23:26, God assured His people of longevity; and promised that He will fulfill the number of their days.

Every one of us has allotted number of years to live, right from creation. We are given to live long. Those who die untimely death are those who have failed to fulfill the number of days assigned to them. The major factor that brings premature death is sin. But God's original plan and design is long life for His people. God meant for us to fulfill our days.

Isa. 65:20, 22

> **20 "No more shall an infant from there live but a few days, nor an old man who has not fulfilled his days; for the child shall die one hundred years old, but the sinner being one hundred years old shall be accursed.**
>
> **22 They shall not build and another inhabit; they shall not plant and another eat; for as the days of a tree, so shall be the days of My people, and My elect shall long enjoy the work of their hands.**

"… as the days of a tree, so shall be the days of My people…" Thus says the Lord. This speaks about long and fruitful life.

If God's prescription for Israel His servants is long life, how much then would be for believers, who are His adopted children (Rom 8:14-17).

Psalm 91:14-16 gives us further assurances of long life. It talks about the promises that await those who have set their hearts to love God.

A believer is counted as one who has set his love upon the Lord. The Bible says he who hates sin, who obeys Jesus' commands, is he who loves God (Ps 97:10). And the covenant blessing or reward for him is that, God will HONOR HIM AND SATISFY HIM WITH LONG LIFE.

It is believer's right to enjoy a long fruitful life here on earth (Ps 91:16), and eternity bliss in heaven (John 10:28; Rev. 2:7; 22:14).

Therefore, as a believer, stand on the Word of God, walk with God, and begin to claim your inheritance - divine health and long life.

CHAPTER 4

Wealth and Prosperity

Once, I heard a denominational preacher say on a TV program that, God created the poor to test the rich. By extension, that seems to suggest that God is the author/creator of poverty. Can this postulation be a scriptural truth or scriptural fallacy?

In the first place, the above statement is everything but the truth. I mean, it's far from the truth. I will show that subsequently.

The Bible tells us in the book of Genesis (1:31) that everything God created was good. Is poverty good?

Remember, the epistle of James says that, every good and every perfect gift comes from God (Jas. 1:17). You will agree with me, poverty does not meet the qualification of good and perfect gift. Poverty is an obnoxious and distasteful thing.

Moreover, we learnt from the accounts of the Bible that, there are three principal curses of the law – the curse of sickness, the curse of poverty and curse of spiritual death (Deut. 28:15-63). These are curses that befall the people who disobey the commands of God. Poverty, therefore, is not a blessing but a curse.

When Jesus went to the cross, these are the curses of the law which He delivered us (believers) from. Satan is the author of sin, and of course, poverty (Gal. 3:13-14).

Author of Prosperity

Who is the author of prosperity? To whom do the wealth and the riches of this world belong? Whose possessions are the gold and silver of the earth?

Psalm 24:1 says all the earth and all its fullness are owned by God.

What is the fullness of the earth? It is all the material and mineral resources on the earth and right under the belly of the earth.

The Scriptures further add, that every beast of the forest, and very silver and gold of the earth, all belong to God (Ps. 50:10-12; Hag. 2:8).

God the Father owns all. I ask, if your father is rich and wealthy (a man of great means), what should you expect as your inheritance? Poverty or prosperity?

In the gospel of Luke chapter fifteen, when the prodigal son walked up to his father, what claims did he make? He made a demand on the father's wealth not on his poverty.

God our Father owns everything, and He is the Author of true prosperity.

Power to Make Wealth

God has demonstrated again and again that He delights to bless His people with riches and wealth.

First, from the beginning when He created Adam, He gave Adam the ownership, and charge of the earth. But Adam committed high treason, and sold out to Satan. Right now Satan is in control of the wealth of the earth, as the god of the earth (2 Cor. 4:4).

Consider the Patriarchs, Abraham, Isaac and Jacob. They were all men of great means. God blessed them and prospered them greatly. Even in difficult times, they multiplied in resources, and waxed great, and became exceedingly prosperous (Gen. 26:12-14).

The prosperity of God's people is expressly the design and the will of God. God did not only desire and designed it, He adequately provided for it. He did not put all the gold and silver in the earth for the children of disobedience, but rather for His people.

As we were told from the Bible, the children of Jacob had served Egypt for 430 years in abject poverty, sorrow, denial and deprivation. And thereafter, God worked out their release in a dramatic and miraculous way.

In the night of their departure from Egypt, God gave Israel unusual favor in the sight of the Egyptians; they received divine-mediated compensation for their labor of many years (Exod. 12:35-36).

The psalmist puts it in a very interesting way. He says, God brought them out with silver and gold. There is no gainsaying the fact that prosperity is God's design for His people.

Secondly, God did not only give children of Israel favor to get wealth, He also gave them power to prosper, as they advanced to settle in the Promised Land.

Deut. 8:18 (NIV)

> **18 But remember the Lord your God, for it is he who gives you the ability to produce wealth, and so confirms his covenant, which he swore to your forefathers, as it is today.**

Note what the Scriptures say in the above texts, that God gives His people the ability, power to prosper (to get or produce wealth). One interesting aspect of this Scripture is the mention of the word covenant.

We said earlier that a covenant is an agreement that demands and fulfills a commitment.

You would remember back at Genesis chapter 22 when Abraham wholeheartedly obeyed God, God made a covenant with Abraham to bless him and prosper him and all his descendants after him. God swore a covenant of prosperity to Abraham,

Gen. 22:15-18

15 Then the Angel of the Lord called to Abraham a second time out of heaven,

16 and said:" By Myself I have sworn, says the Lord, because you have done this thing, and have not withheld your son, your only son —

17 blessing I will bless you, and will multiply your descendants as the stars of the heaven and as the sand which is on the seashore; and your descendants shall possess the gate of their enemies.

18 In your seed all the nations of the earth shall be blessed, because you have obeyed My voice."

Let's look at Deuteronomy eighth chapter again Why does God give His people power to prosper? That He may fulfill and establish for His people the covenant of prosperity which He swore to Abraham His servant.

So we can say God *covenantly* determined to bless His people. Note that there is nowhere in all the Scriptures where God gave His people poverty or power to fail. Poverty is evil. Poverty is not from God. Those who are teaching that God created the poor to test the rich are those propagating the doctrine of demons. They are miss-educating and misleading the people.

God gives His people the power to get wealth because it's His design and will that His people prosper and be wealthy. He does not make some rich and others poor. His blessings are for all – for everyone who fulfill the terms of the covenant.

That's why Prophet Isaiah says that God's blessings belong to those who are willing and would obey (Isa. 1:19).

If you are obedient you are granted to prosper. To eat the good of the land is to prosper. The good of the land means the best things of life and living. Is this Scripture addressed to a select few? No, it speaks to everyone who will obey. God does not have favorites nor does He show partiality (Acts 10:34).

If as the Bible says, God rejoices to do us good and multiply us (Deut. 28:63a), then it must, without doubt, be His purpose and plan to prosper us His children.

Back in the wilderness, Moses assured the children of Jacob of God's resolve to prosper them; saying to them that God will command His blessings upon them and cause His uncommon favor to overtake them, if they would obey Him always (Deut. 28:1-2, 8-11).

Our Prosperity – God's Pleasure

Some folks find it difficult to believe that God has promised and planned to make us rich. Against the risk of being misunderstood, let me make the following clarifications.

First, it's God's promise to make us rich. Being rich does not necessarily mean we will become millionaires. Being rich means having a full supply; it means having all your needs met. Even if you don't have millions in monetary terms but all your needs are met, you are rich (of course, some would have millions in financial terms).

Secondly, we cannot all be rich equally or at same time. All the mangoes on the tree do not ripen the same day.

Our prosperity is relative, and it comes at diverse times, subject to our faith, and our readiness to walk with God.

But believe this, God has pleasure in our prosperity, and has promised to make us rich.

In Jer. 29:11 God says He has plans to bless and prosper His people. He calls them plans of peace; good plans to prosper us and not to hurt us.

Isn't it exciting? That God has plans for us – good plans. Not a plan of evil or disaster but plans to prosper us. This is the true Word of God. God does not 'bless' some people with poverty to test the rich. That's demonic dogma.

Another version says I have good plans for you; not plans to hurt you. Prosperity does not hurt. But poverty obviously does; it sure hurts. Proverb 10:15 says poverty destroys.

Your well-being and prosperity is God's design – His eternal will and delight. David the sweet psalmist of Israel, speaking under divine inspiration, assured us of this in Psalm chapter thirty-five

Ps. 35:27 confirms that God has pleasure in our prosperity. In other words, God rejoices to do us good, bless us with prosperity, and also rejoices to see us enjoy it. That's what the totality of that verse pictures.

One particular version of that psalm puts a more refreshing note to that verse when it says God delights in the well-being of his servants.

I ask again, what is it that has capacity to work out a man's well-being, prosperity or poverty? Would God who has keen interest and delight in my well-being rather give me poverty instead of prosperity? Beware of the lying tongues and deceiving spirits that abound in this end time. Let nobody deceive you or talk you out of your inheritance, it is God's will that you prosper.

The blessing of the Lord is what confers riches and wealth. Prosperity comes from divine blessing while poverty comes from curse. Poverty causes sorrow (Prov. 10:22).

Throughout the Old Testament, God has always shown His eagerness to bless His people with riches (Isa. 60:1-2, 5, 11, 15-17).

Prosperity – Believers' Right

Under the New Testament dispensation, prosperity is the right of the children of God (believers). The psalmist says the fullness of the earth belongs to God (Ps. 24:1). Believers being children of God, and heirs of God (joint-heirs with Christ), are the beneficiaries of the wealth of the earth

(Rom. 8:15-17). Believers, therefore, will inherit wealth and prosperity, and not poverty.

The good news about it all is that believers' prosperity is a settled matter. Ps. 119:89 says God's Word is settled forever in heaven.

It's so because God's word says He gives His people power to prosper, as it's His plan and design that they succeed and not fail. And the Scriptures say, the Word of God cannot be broken (John 10:35).

Furthermore, Second Corinthians 8:9 tells us how this matter is settled.

2 Cor. 8:9

> **9 For you know the grace of our Lord Jesus Christ, that though He was rich, yet for your sakes He became poor, that you through His poverty might become rich.**

Jesus made Himself poor that believers may become rich. Jesus was rich but He accepted poverty, and became poor in order to promote believers to prosperity. How sweet!

This is a great act of generosity (using the word of another version of the Bible). Jesus made Himself poor to make a believer rich. Being richly blessed out of Christ poverty is both spiritual and material – I should say it's an all-round provision.

3 John 2

2 Beloved, I pray that you may prosper in all things and be in health, just as your soul prospers.

It's a whole scale provision. The riches accruing to a believer out of Jesus poverty is all-encompassing – *be in health* (physical prosperity); *prosper in all things* (material); *as your soul prospers* (spiritual prosperity). Believers' right to prosperity is a settled matter.

The epistle of third John speaks of a divine provision that is ready-made for believers. A believer has a right to all-round settlement, as it were.

God has the capability to provide for our needs (Phil. 4:19). How many needs will God supply? ALL, it says. If all your needs are supplied, then indeed you are rich. This is your settlement – your claim as a believer.

God is with us to do us good, and multiply us. He gave us His only begotten Son to settle the matter of our salvation – the best gift there could be. If He did this, the Bible asks, will *He not with Him also freely give us all things?* (Rom. 8:32).

All things, I believe strongly, means all blessings – every available blessing; here and now, and also in eternity.

And of course, all things exclude sickness, failure, poverty, demotion and other forms of darkness. These are not blessings, but rather curses of the law (Deut. 28:15-63).

Accompanying Condition

From the foregoing, we have been able to prove that it's God's will and plan to prosper believers. We have also been able to establish that believers have right to prosperity as their inheritance in Christ.

But inheritances are subject to rules, regulations and conditions. For instance, if a man receives an inheritance but was later discovered not to be the legal son of the testator or not his rightful heir or does not bear the name he claims, he would certainly lose his rights or claim.

God in Christ has blessed us with covenant of prosperity, and has given us the right to prosper. But there are conditions to fulfill.

First, to enjoy the right to prosper, one must be born again (that is become a believer) -John 1:12-13.

Only believers are children of God, and can exercise or use that right. And the Bible says the Holy Spirit confirms that believers are children of God. And because God is their Father, believers have become heirs of God (joint-heirs with Christ) – Rom. 8:16-17. The heir-ship confers on the believer the right to prosper.

If you are not born again, you are not a child of God (John 1:12; 1 John 3:10). Therefore, you have no inheritance in Christ.

Secondly, your right to prosper is dependent upon the quality of your spiritual life and walk with God. God commanded

Abraham to walk before Him blameless. Likewise, you must live a holy life – be imitator of God, walking in love. Two cannot partner together except they are in agreement. And Prov. 28:13 caps it all by saying that, anyone who dwells in sins will not prosper.

You need to have fruitful, quality fellowship with God to key into His divine provisions (Josh 1:8; Ps 1:1-3).

Thirdly, obedience is a major key to the blessings of God. Abraham obeyed, and God did for Abraham what He has never done to any mortal – He swore by His name to Abraham a covenant of blessing, multiplication and prosperity (Gen. 22:16-18). That was awesome.

If you are obedient to God, you will eat the good of the land (Isa. 1:19). The good of the land are all the covenant blessings of God – the wealth and riches and prosperity God has prepared for His heritage (believers in Christ). All these come on the wing of obedience. I make bold to say, obedience is the key to all the blessings of God.

Moses reminded the children of Israel again and again, how far and how high obedience can carry them. There are no limits.

Deut. 28:1-2

> **"Now it shall come to pass, if you diligently obey the voice of the Lord your God, to observe carefully all His commandments which I**

command you today, that the Lord your God will set you high above all nations of the earth.

2 And all these blessings shall come upon you and overtake you, because you obey the voice of the Lord your God:

To enjoy the covenant of prosperity, obey the Scriptural principles of prosperity. These principles are enunciated in the following excerpts.

Prov. 11:24-25

> **24 There is one who scatters, yet increases more; and there is one who withholds more than is right, but it leads to poverty.**
>
> **25 The generous soul will be made rich, and he who waters will also be watered himself.**

To increase, that is to prosper, you must scatter. What does it mean to scatter? It means to give, to share, to sow.

Luke 6:38

> **38 Give, and it will be given to you: good measure, pressed down, shaken together, and running over will be put into your bosom. For with the same measure that you use, it will be measured back to you."**

What are we to give? Give to God, offering, tithes, first fruits (Deut. 16:16-17; Malachi 3:8-12; Prov. 3:9-10). It also means to give to church and church programs (Zech. 1:17); to give to needy folks (Prov. 19:17; Gal 6:10; Rom. 12:13).

Giving is sowing. There is not a farmer who sows without a harvest. I have this on the authority of Word of God.

As God says in Gen. 8:22, seedtime and harvest time will not cease on the earth until the end of all things.

As we see in the Scriptures, prosperity goes with sowing. The one, who sows bountifully, will reap bountifully (2 Cor. 9:6-11).

Sowing engenders multiplication, and brings rich harvest of prosperity. It ensures sufficiency, and delivers abundance for good works in the kingdom of God.

Don't ever stop sowing. It is the key to the believer's right to prosper. Diligent farmers have assurance of harvest.

Believers exercising due diligence of obedience are prosperity farmers. Your claim to prosperity is a settled matter.

Precept upon Precept

Proverb 24:5 says a man of knowledge is a man power. Every blessing of our lives is Word-based. And our access to these blessings is dependent on the quality and volume of Word of God in our lives (knowledge), and our obedience thereof.

Isa. 28:9-10

> **9 "Whom will he teach knowledge? And whom will he make to understand the message? Those just weaned from milk? Those just drawn from the breasts?**

> **10 For precept must be upon precept, precept upon precept, Line upon line, line upon line, Here a little, there a little."**

Precept must be upon precept. Getting proper perspective and understanding of God's Word determines how far you will walk with God.

Some have argued, if God did not create poverty, why is there so much poverty in our world? Is there anything on earth God did not create?

They look at some Scriptures as their conviction and comfort. God who created light also created darkness. So they reason, He must also be author of all – both the good, the bad, the ugly, the evil. Take this as an example.

Isa 45:6-7

> **6 That they may know from the rising of the sun to its setting that there is none besides Me. I am the Lord, and there is no other;**

7 I form the light and create darkness, I make peace and create calamity; I, the Lord, do all these things.'

Other versions refer to God as the One who brings peace and causes trouble or brings prosperity and creates disaster or makes harmony and creates disorder or doom.

Some have argued stridently that *poverty, trouble, calamity, disaster, doom, disorder and evil* are all on the same page. In other words, poverty is evil just as well disaster, calamity, trouble and doom. If God created all these, who also formed the light, then He also created the evil called poverty. I hesitate to concur.

Some also would point me to Job 5:17-18, where it says God chastens. He bruises and binds up; He wounds and makes whole.

Also bruises and wounds are on the same page as trouble, calamity, evil and all that.

Does God do evil? Does He create evil? I say emphatic no.

For, if God did, He will be the doer of evil. But God is God, God is not the devil. We all know Satan is the doer of evil – the devil.

But why does the Bible say God create evil? Remember the initial testimony of the Bible that everything God created was INDEED VERY GOOD (Gen. 1:31). Good is not evil, and evil is not good. Evil is evil. Good is good. Good is the direct opposite of evil.

If everything God created was very good, God then could not have been the creator of evil (or everything that is evil). God is not the author, nor the creator of evil. Satan is! Evil came into the world through Satan (via his unholy alliance with Adam/Eve).

Why then does the Bible variously pen that God created evil? Please note this. We must endeavor to ensure that precept must be upon precept.

Though the Bible says what it means, and means also what it says, interpretation of verse(s) must take into cognizance the preceding and the following verses, as well as the original language of the Bible, and its dialectical variables, and also its socio-cultural setting.

The writer of Isa. 45:7 sought unambiguously to ascribe the power and the government and the glory of all things to God, and God alone (not to idols, nor chance), nor to any subordinate cause. Everything (success or adversity) is traceable entirely to God.

God created light and darkness (darkness is the result when He takes light away). Light is also the emblem of good and anything good like peace and prosperity. Darkness is the emblem of what is bad like war and adversity.

But all things whether good or bad (evil) like prosperity or adversity are all under the providential control and direction of God. God either ordained or permitted them (Rom. 1:26, 28).

God makes peace and creates evil, as the Bible says (Isa. 45::7). Evil here means that which is the opposite of peace; for instance, war or calamity. So God makes peace, and could also permit or order war or calamity or trouble or doom, to beat His people back on the track. Everything peace or trouble or calamity are entirely under the direction and ordering of His Providence.

Given the socio-cultural circumstances of Israel at that time, Bible scholars appear to be in agreement that evil so referred, is not moral darkness (sin).

Take particular note of epistle of James 1:13, which says *"Let no one say when he is tempted, "I am tempted by God"; for God cannot be tempted by evil, nor does He Himself tempt anyone"*

God is a supernatural Being who is infinitely and absolutely good. If God cannot be tempted by evil, and He Himself does not tempt anyone, then God is not the author of moral darkness (sin). Satan is.

Isa. 45:7 is like First Samuel 16:14, which described King Saul as being visited by a distressing spirit from the Lord.

God is infinitely pure and holy, and cannot harbor evil spirit (distressing spirit). As a king anointed by God, the Holy Spirit dwelled with Saul. But the day he rebelled against God, and parted ways with God, the Holy Spirit

departed from him, and God permitted (or ordered) the evil spirit that troubled Saul. God did not make the evil spirits. Everything God created from the beginning was very good. The perversion (evil) that came on the way was not made by God.

So, God may permit evil (poverty, calamity, doom, war etc.) if need be, because all things answer to His providential direction and ordering.

God does not do evil, and He is not the architect of evil. Iniquity and wickedness are none of His. But He gives to man his due according to his seed – good for good sown and evil (permitted) for evil sown.

In conclusion, we state that, God did not create the poor in order to test the rich. Believers have right to prosperity under the new covenant, purchased by Christ's blood on the Calvary cross.

Whether or not a believer will enjoy this covenant or inheritance depends on his fellowship with God; and also on his knowledge, and understanding of the promises of God and his right/authority in Christ, and his ability to stand on God's Word (faith).

CHAPTER 5

Protection and Security

The psalmist David cried out to God, perhaps out of distress, perceived insecurity, danger or fear. It was a heartfelt prayer for protection over one on whom danger looms large.

Ps. 17:7-9

> **7 Show Your marvelous lovingkindness by Your right hand, O You who save those who trust in You from those who rise up against them.**
>
> **8 Keep me as the apple of Your eye; Hide me under the shadow of Your wings,**
>
> **9 From the wicked who oppress me, from my deadly enemies who surround me.**

Take note of the expression, *"under the shadow of your wings"*. What a great hiding place! What a secured fortress! If the Almighty (the Keeper of Israel, who does not slumber nor sleep), keeps you, you are forever secure.

We are all in need of God's mercy, protection, preservation and security. And God Himself knows this.

Deut. 33:12

> **12 Of Benjamin he said: "The beloved of the Lord shall dwell in safety by Him, Who shelters him all the daylong; and he shall dwell between His shoulders."**

Hear that assurance: *the beloved of the Lord shall dwell in safety, secured all day long.*

We see the proof of the above all over the Scriptures. The Patriarchs, Abraham, Isaac and Jacob, sojourned in the wilderness of Canaan land for decades, faced with diverse threats, insecurity, dangers and the hostilities of men of the land. Attempts were made twice to snatch beautiful brides. Wells were contended and seized.

At a particular point, war had to be fought (Gen. 14:1-16). But through all these, the beloved of the Lord (the Patriarchs) were granted maximum protection and security.

God loves His own, and would do anything to keep them as the apple of His eye, above all hurts, threats and danger.

Regarding this, I must say I love the cheer and confidence of the Psalmist David in the following verses.

Ps. 5:11-12

> **11 But let all those rejoice who put their trust in You; Let them ever shout for joy, because You**

defend them; Let those also who love Your name be joyful in You.

12 For You, O Lord, will bless the righteous; with favor You will surround him as with a shield.

The favor of God is our shield of protection that makes us dwell in safety and security.

God has shown it repeatedly that He is the hiding place for His people; the secret place of His presence is their fortress from trouble and foes alike.

The Bible is replete with testimonies of God's protection and deliverance, and security for His beloved servants. To us believers, God is our secret hiding place. In Him we are preserved from all troubles, to sing continually songs of deliverance (Ps. 32:7; 27:5-6).

Recall the 430 years sojourn in Egypt – the hardship, the oppression, the sorrow, the subjugation, the dehumanizing labor and bondage. In all these, God watched over them protectively from afar, as it were. He did not forget His promise to Abraham His friend. He preserved His chosen people by His tender mercies and loving-kindness (Ps. 40:11), and did not deliver them to the will of their enemies (Ps. 41:2).

I am also reminded of the spectacular deliverance of Israel from the iron-grip of Pharaoh. God by His mighty power had brought them out from the house of bondage, and headed them toward the Promised Land.

Even when the Red Sea resisted and reproached them while their enemies gleefully charged from the rear, God looked from heaven with derision and scorn at Pharaoh and his troop. He knew they were on a fatalistic pursuit – a journey of no return. God stood in defense of His people. He surrounded them, and led them by His angels (Ps. 91:11).

Yes, He gave His angels charge over Israel against the rampaging, bloody host of pursuing Egyptian soldiers. And thereafter, all the way to the Promised Land, He gave them uncommon and spectacular protection; and direction by the pillar of fire by night, and the pillar of cloud by day, along with the host of angels. They had security even against snakes and other wild beasts of the wilderness.

Believer's Right to Protection

Throughout the Old Testament, God's resolve to protect and defend His people had always been palpable to all. The dramatic release of Israel from Egypt after the national disaster of the death of every first born of the Egyptians, and the miraculous cross walk of the Red Sea, were familiar stories to all the nations of Canaan land. Israel was highly respected and feared, on the accounts of these dumbfounding miracles.

God put all the nations on notice regarding His servants, Israel. God permitted no one to harm them, and He rebuked nations for their sakes. He fought and destroyed nations for His people (Ps. 105:13-15 KJV).

In demonstrating His continual faithfulness to Israel, God charged all, men and beasts alike, to honor and defer to His people. Hosea 2:18 says,

> **18 In that day I will make a covenant for them with the beasts of the field, with the birds of the air, And with the creeping things of the ground. Bow and sword of battle I will shatter from the earth, to make them lie down safely.**

God made a covenant of protection and security on behalf of His people to keep them in perpetual safety. This is an act of great grace and mercy. If He did these for the children of Israel His servant, how much more do you reckon He would do for believers, who are His adopted children?

The Psalmist says a man who is planted in the house of the Lord will prosper. Who are those planted in the house of the Lord? The believers! This is what the spiritual experience and blessings of regeneration (new birth) engenders. He who is born of the Spirit is planted in the house of the Lord because the Trinity makes their home in him (John 14:23). And, flourishing and succeeding in life affairs, takes cognizance of security. One can only flourish in a protected and secured environment.

Believers have better covenant founded on better promises. There is a covenant of protection and security over the believer for which Jesus Christ is the surety (Heb. 7:22; 8:6). As a Christian, you have an inalienable right to divine protection and security procured by Christ's work of redemption at the cross.

In the first place, Bible scholars say the word *salvation* in Hebrew and Greek implies *deliverance, preservation, safety, healing and soundness.* These accommodate the concept of believers' protection and security.

Let's consider one spectacular testimony in Acts chapter twelve. Herod the king had killed James the brother of John. Because this pleased the Jews, he also arrested Peter and kept him under maximum security, to be killed after the Passover feast.

On the eve of Peter's execution, an angel of the Lord came into the prison, and led Peter out, in the midst of four squads of guard soldiers. And so Peter escaped from the hand of Herod and his evil plan. (Acts 12:1-19).

Believers are God's vessels of mercy and not vessels of wrath (Rom. 9:22-23). Therefore, God's covenant of protection and security preserves them from danger, and from every destruction. God's mercy upholds them continually.

Another strange testimony is recorded in Acts chapter sixteen. Paul and Silas had been arrested, and severely beaten, and imprisoned, chained to stocks. At midnight, as they prayed and praised God, there was an earthquake that collapsed the walls of the prison, broke loose their chains, and set them free (Acts 16:16-34).

Protection and security are believers' right (their covenant blessings). Indeed, it's so because, like Peter or Paul, a believer is kept through the power of God, and in the mighty name of God (John 17:11-12).

The name of the Lord is a strong tower (Prov. 18:10), and we are kept by that mighty name.

As believers, we have divine protection against Satan and demons (Ps. 91:13, Luke 10:19; 1 John 5:18); against evil arrows and pestilences (Ps. 91:3-6; 1 Pet. 2:24); against physical disasters and elements.

I heard a testimony of a man of God who had boarded a commuter bus for a distant journey. A short while after the bus drove off the park, he heard a voice (or a command rather). The voice said, 'come down' (something like that). And he looked around to see who was speaking but everyone around him appeared to have slept. He then informed the driver he was no longer travelling, and would like to alight. The driver and others in the bus were somewhat angry at him but they let him alight. About three hours into the journey, the vehicle had a flat tire, and ended up in the bush in flames, and everyone therein died.

God keeps His own, the believer; and He does it in style - in ways we cannot decipher. The early Disciples of Christ had full assurance that God will deliver them from every evil work and keep them for His heavenly kingdom.

This was the confidence of Apostle Paul in his ministry. I feel this same confidence, and bold trust reverberating through my system. Is this not the confidence believers have in the Lord, who purchased our salvation (protection and security inclusive), with His own blood (1 Cor. 6:20; Acts 20:28)

The Psalmist says the man who dwells in the secret place of the Most High God, will surely abide under the shadow of the Almighty God.

And I am sure Psalm 91 is talking all about you the believer. If you are born again, you are dwelling under the secret place, under the shadow of the Almighty. Please read, and pray this psalm again and again.

CHAPTER 6

Fruitfulness and Success

Right from the creation works, man was made a fruitful being with a gem of success and greatness. There was no barrenness in man or failure. The originating word that created man was clothed in awesome power, dynamism and fruitfulness.

When God created the lower creatures of the earth, He gave them the divine endowment of fruitfulness, and commanded them to be fruitful, to multiply and fill the earth (Gen 1:22-23).

The same command was what God gave to Adam, though at a higher level. God empowered them (in the wordings of the Bible, *God blessed them*), and commanded them to be fruitful and successful. Fruitfulness, multiplication and success were the initial goals God set for them. Failure was never part of the mandate. Failure came through Satan. The curse of barrenness and failure came as a result of the fall. But, God's original purpose was fruitfulness and success.

Gen. 1:28

> **28 Then God blessed them, and God said to them, "Be fruitful and multiply; fill the earth and subdue it; have dominion over the fish of**

the sea, over the birds of the air, and over every living thing that moves on the earth."

God's purpose and plan for man, the jewel of His creation, is fruitfulness and success. His heart toward man is love. Even when He appeared to Jacob, He blessed him with the blessing of fruitfulness (Gen. 35:11-12).

God is always with His people to bless them, and to grant success to their work (Gen. 39:23). And after the death of Joseph, when the children of Israel were settled in Egypt, God continued to bless and empower them to succeed. The Bible said the children of Jacob were fruitful; they multiplied and grew exceedingly mighty in the land (Exod. 1:6-7).

God's plan for man's success is an all-encompassing one. He has made plans for man to be fruitful physically and materially. Beginning early, He promised the children of Israel great future. None were to cast their young or be barren (Exod. 23:25-26).

Concerning this topic, Jeremiah captured God's plan vividly in the following verse

Jer. 17:7-8

> **7 "Blessed is the man who trusts in the Lord, and whose hope is the Lord.**
>
> **8 For he shall be like a tree planted by the waters, which spreads out its roots by the river, And will not fear when heat comes; But its leaf will be**

green, And will not be anxious in the year of drought, Nor will cease from yielding fruit.

When God created Adam, he became God's partner. God entrusted to Adam all His works on the earth, giving Adam dominion and control over them, and the administratorship. God gave Adam all the investiture of power to be successful in that assignment. But that partnership came tragically to an end when Adam sinned.

Adam breached the law. Even at that, God's mercy did not depart from man entirely.

Though, Abraham and Sarah had reproductive challenges, the grace and mercy of God worked out a divine intervention that brought laughter into their lives.

It was same token that gave the children of Jacob exceeding fruitfulness in Egypt, that saw them grew from just 70 people to over one million people in a space of time (Exod. 1:7).

The children of Jacob, as the covenant people of God, have always enjoyed exceeding fruitfulness, on the account of God's covenant with Abraham.

Believers in Christ have a share in the blessings of Abraham. Abraham is the father of faith (Rom. 4:16-18)).

Jesus Christ is a descendant of David (Jer. 23:5, 6; Isa. 11:1-2), who himself is a descendant of Abraham. Believers as spiritual Jews (Rom. 2:28-29), are also children of Abraham. This is so because of our association with Christ, through the new birth. And being seeds of Abraham by our standing in Christ, all the covenant blessings of Abraham are ours.

The Bible says Christ, by His death and resurrection has delivered us (believers) from the curses of the law; and by the exceeding riches of His grace, has also made us beneficiaries of the covenant blessings of Abraham. By this token, we are both Abraham's seed and heirs, according to the promise made to him by God (Gal. 3:13-14, 29).

Some might argue that fruitfulness is not an exclusive right of believers. In terms of physical (bodily) fruitfulness, it seems to them that unbelievers are as fruitful as believers.

So it seems. Yet there is a significant difference. Even God promised Hagar that He would multiply her descendants exceedingly (Gen 16:10). Yet, there is a difference. A vital difference exists between the believer and the unbeliever, in terms of fruitfulness.

First, the covenant blessing of Abraham was not passed on to Ishmael or to his descendants. It was the sole right of Isaac and his descendants (Jacob and his children), and to believers who became also the seeds of Abraham by their faith in Christ (Gal. 3:26, 29).

Secondly, the Bible says, God seeks *godly offspring* (Mal. 2:15). Godly offspring comes only from believers. Being fruitful is not an end in itself. From where does God get glory? It's from godly offspring of His elect believers (Isa. 8:18). God Himself calls them elect, holy and beloved (Col. 3:12).

Thirdly, God says of the believers, in Isa. 65:23 that they shall not be fruitful for evil or in vain, or with cursed seeds: they shall not bring forth children for trouble. In other words, their children shall not be for shame or reproach or for failure. On the contrary, the result of their fruitfulness shall be blessed seeds of the Lord. Their children shall be for glory – for signs and wonders (Isa. 8:18).

Moreover, fruitfulness goes beyond the physical realm (bodily fruitfulness). There is also material fruitfulness – this, talks about multiplication and increase in means of wealth; about success in life.

As we saw in the previous chapters, God promised to prosper and make His children successful (that is material prosperity), as part of Abraham blessings. Abraham was blessed bodily (in multitudes of descendants) as well as material possessions. In other words, he was fruitful physically and materially (Gen. 24:35).

Some might also contend that unbelievers control amazing material wealth in this world. It's not surprising because their father Satan is controlling the finances of the world (excluding, of course, believers' finances). He is a thief. Remember, the earth and all its fullness belong to God, our Father.

Unbelievers may be controlling great wealth in the world today, but the Bible assures us that the wealth of sinners belongs to the righteous (Prov. 13:22). Don't be surprised. Sooner or later there will be wealth transfer from the hand of the unjust to the children of God.

God does not get glory from whatever amazing material wealth that is on the side of unbelievers. The wealth of the unbelievers is doomed (Ps. 92:6-7).

Yes, they wicked may flourish (that is, enjoying exceeding material fruitfulness), but they shall be destroyed forever. True, enduring wealth (kingdom prosperity) is the right of believers. Good success and prosperous ways are on the side of believers (Josh. 1:8)

Spiritual Fruitfulness

There is another dimension of fruitfulness concept – spiritual fruitfulness. According to the Word of God in the third epistle of John, believers have promise of all round fruitfulness.

Everyone who is born again has entered the arena of spiritual fruitfulness. And believers are to *bear fruits worthy of repentance.* (Matt. 3:8). This is a right of every believer.

Bearing worthy fruits goes beyond good conduct and godly lifestyle (Gal. 5:22-23). It is about reproducing the life of God that is in us, in others (unbelievers). It is about soul winning. Jesus declared that it is soul winning that will make a believer truly fruitful, and that will keep him alive (John 15:1-2).

A branch that refuses or fails to bear fruit is taken away (cut off). Can a branch cut off, keep or maintain life? No!

A believer must bear fruit (win souls into the kingdom of God); it's a believer's right to bear fruit.

It's the delight of God that a believer bears fruit because it is a divine channel of blessing for him. (God has pleasure to bless His people). Soul winning makes for further fruitfulness, success and answers to prayers (verse 16).

Here is God's guarantee for answered prayers: when we win souls, whatever you ask the Father in Jesus' name, will be granted to us

Believers have right to divine fruitfulness and success.

CHAPTER 7

Freedom

Man was created free – a free moral agent. But Adam, perhaps, thought he was exercising his freedom when he made an evil choice that truncated his liberty and destiny. The moment he disobeyed God, he lost his freedom, and brought himself under Satan's captivity and government.

So many people think they have freedom, but unknown to them, they are under certain captivity. That was the story of the Pharisees at the time of Christ ministry on the earth. They argued with Jesus Christ that they were children of Abraham, that they were free people who had never been in bondage to anyone. But Jesus tried to make them realize that they were under bondage to Satan. He who sins is a slave of sin (John 8:15-36).

There are two forms of bondage – physical and spiritual. Israel's 430 years stay in Egypt is an example of physical bondage.

Our focus here is the latter (spiritual bondage). A man may be free (not being in jail, or not being a slave or servant of another), but as long as he is a sinner, his freedom is partial or limited. Many people in life are living under partial freedom.

Spiritual bondage is the worst form of bondage. A lot of people in such situation do not even realize they are under spiritual bondage (like the Pharisees).

Gate to Freedom

Freedom is a property of life - a God-given possession. The whole of humanity came under bondage because of the sin of Adam and Eve (John 8:34).

But, how can a man come out of captivity? Only by embracing Christ.

The Bible says Christ has delivered us from the curse of the law (Gal. 3:13). Bondage is one of the effects of curse of the law; they came as a result of sin

Jesus Christ is the only One who has the power to deliver man from spiritual bondage. He delivered man (who believes in Him) from the bondage of Satan – Satan's prison. The Bible shows that Satan has a prison, where he detains men who are in his kingdom (Isa 14:17).

But Jesus Christ perfected the freedom of man by His death and resurrection (through the sacrifice of His blood on the cross). – Rom. 6:17, 18.

To come out of Satan's prison, you need to surrender your life to Jesus Christ – confess and accept Him as Lord and Savior (Rom. 10:9, 10).

Christ is He who procured freedom for humanity (John 3:15-20; Rom. 6:22). The Bible says we were bought at a price (1 Cor. 6:20). God purchased our freedom with the precious blood of Jesus Christ. He is the gate-way to liberty.

You cannot claim to be free and enjoying true liberty if you don't have Christ in your life.

Christ is the beginning of freedom for all men. Know Him and believe in Him, and you would enter into the realm of unlimited freedom. God through Christ has perfected man's freedom.

A believer has right to freedom. Christians are called to liberty, and not to bondage (Gal. 5:13; Rom. 8:15). Freedom or liberty is one of the rights and privileges of Christians. Christ has freed you as a believer from bondage to sin and Satan; you have freedom now in Christ. And as a believer, learn to stand on the liberty, which Christ has purchased for us by His blood.

Freedom Begets Authority

In the original plan of creation, Adam was next to the God-head. Satan was under Adam, who had all authority on the earth (Gen. 1:28; Ps. 8:4-6).

And Adam was the god of the earth. But, after Adam committed high treason, and sold out to Satan, he lost all the authority he had. Adam became a subject of Satan; and so all his descendants.

But thank God for His indescribable gift, Jesus Christ (John 3:16; 2 Cor. 9:15). Jesus Christ by His death and resurrection overturned the table against Satan, and stripped him of the authority he usurped from Adam. Jesus defeated, disarmed and dethroned all satanic forces in His conquest.

Col 2:14-15

> **14 having wiped out the handwriting of requirements that was against us, which was contrary to us. And He has taken it out of the way, having nailed it to the cross.**

> **15 Having disarmed principalities and powers, He made a public spectacle of them, triumphing over them in it.**

Christ's victory over Satan belongs to us believers. His triumph was established by His resurrection from the dead. In His rising, Christ took us (believers) up with Him, from being under-dogs under Satan's authority and rule, as sinners, and promoted us to enjoy His power and glory (Eph. 2:4-6).

God in raising Jesus Christ from the dead quickened us, and gave us new life; and *made us sit together in heavenly places in Christ Jesus.*

The heavenly place is the place of power and authority, above Satan and his cohorts. Believers are seated where Christ is seated. And if Satan is under Christ, (and yes indeed he is), then Satan is under a believer. The Scriptures confirm this.

Eph. 1:20-23

20 which He worked in Christ when He raised Him from the dead and seated Him at His right hand in the heavenly places,

21 far above all principality and power and might and dominion, and every name that is named, not only in this age but also in that which is to come.

22 And He put all things under His feet, and gave Him to be head over all things to the church,

23 which is His body, the fullness of Him who fills all in all.

Christ's victory is for the church, the body of Christ. If Christ is seated in heavenly places above all powers and principalities, with all things under His feet, that's also where a believer is seated.

A believer by the victory of Christ, and His grace, has authority over Satan and all his works. If you don't know this you will still be walking under Satan's rule, and be subject to all his works (sickness, poverty etc.). But if you know your right and standing in Christ, you can successfully claim and exercise your authority over Satan, situations and circumstances. There's no gain-saying the fact that a believer is a victor not a victim; a believer is a conqueror.

As a believer, you're indeed a conqueror; God has restored you to position of authority above Satan, and has put all things under your feet (by your association with Christ).

To the believer is given the power and authority, and right to trample upon demonic forces and elements (Luke 10:19). What a great privilege!

As a believer, you have right to freedom and victory, and you have Christ's authority over the old dragon. Learn to exercise it, and do exploit in the name of Jesus. This authority is your key to victorious Christian life.

CHAPTER 8

Indwelling Holy Spirit

I n the Old Testament era, the impartation and indwelling of Holy Spirit was a privilege enjoyed only by three categories of people – the kings, the priests and the prophets. Outside this group, none else enjoyed this unique spiritual experience.

King Saul was anointed by God, by the hand of Prophet Samuel, before he became the king (1 Sam. 10:1); and so was David (1 Sam 16:12-13).

Also, Elisha before he became a prophet was anointed (1 Kings 19:15-16).

The anointing of these sets of people demonstrated that they occupy special positions with divine seal. Such impartation positioned them to be effective leaders of the people, and a guide to them.

Priests, kings and prophets are people who have special influence (by reason of God's presence), and the people were to seek after them for divine direction and guidance.

This divine influence is illustrated vividly in First Samuel chapter eighteen the tenth verse, when the Spirit of God departed from King Saul and a distressing spirit took over.

By this, King Saul lost the ability to lead the people of God, and be a guide to them.

Check through the Old Testament, whenever God has a message or instruction for His people, He channels it through their anointed human guide – the prophet or priest or king (mainly the prophet). And God, every now and then, sent His Word to His people through His agents (Ezek. 7:1-2).

The Word of the Lord came to Ezekiel, but not for himself. It was God's instruction to His people. The prophet was a guide to the people. The people inquired of the Lord and sought guide through the prophets.

Spirit Indwelling – Believer's Right

But in the New Testament dispensation, it is entirely a different ball game. One of the many rights and privileges of a believer is the impartation and indwelling presence of Holy Spirit. Every believer has a right to Spirit indwelling. It's a provided right to all men but is conditional upon receiving Jesus Christ first.

The moment a sinner repents and is born again (regenerated, receiving Jesus Christ) he receives immediately the eternal life (John 4:14).

This right did not become effective until Jesus had gone to the cross, died and resurrected from the dead. Even the disciples of Christ did not receive this until after His resurrection as shown in the following Scriptures.

John 14:16-17

16 And I will pray the Father, and He will give you another Helper, that He may abide with you forever —

17 the Spirit of truth, whom the world cannot receive, because it neither sees Him nor knows Him; but you know Him, for He dwells with you and will be in you.

It was through an encounter after His resurrection that the disciples were born again, and received the indwelling Spirit (John 20:21-22). Prior to this, they had a promissory note for their salvation, and the Spirit was with them because Christ was with them.

The purpose of indwelling Spirit partly is to enable a believer build and live heavenly character or lifestyle (that is, bear fruits worthy of repentance) (Gal 5:22-23).

Following the new birth through which we acquire the indwelling Spirit, there is yet a subsequent spiritual experience to which every believer has a right to. This is the baptism with the Holy Spirit (Acts 1:5, 8). Jesus spoke of this in the following Scriptures.

John 7:37-39

37 On the last day, that great day of the feast, Jesus stood and cried out, saying, "If anyone thirsts, let him come to Me and drink.

38 He who believes in Me, as the Scripture has said, out of his heart will flow rivers of living water."

39 But this He spoke concerning the Spirit, whom those believing in Him would receive; for the Holy Spirit was not yet given, because Jesus was not yet glorified.

Jesus Christ gave repeated assurances about the coming of the Holy Spirit (Luke 24:49l Acts 1:5, 8). The Holy Spirit is the promise of the Father, who was come to empower believers and make them effective witnesses of Christ, from Jerusalem to the ends of the earth. And the Spirit came on the day of Pentecost.

The purpose of this outpouring of the Holy Spirit is for service, and to enable us to be a blessing to others. The Holy Spirit through this infilling gives the believers power for service. And by this comes the gifts of the Holy Spirit (1 Cor. 12:4-11), which makes a believer a channel of God's blessings to others.

In my little experience in evangelism, I discovered one disquieting thing. Many Christians do not have knowledge about the baptism of the Holy Spirit. Not many are enjoying this spiritual experience, which is a right of every believer.

Receiving Infilling of Holy Spirit

While the indwelling Spirit is automatic, though conditional upon being born again, the baptism of the Holy Spirit is not automatic. But, it ought to be right after being born again.

What should a believer do to receive this outpouring of the Spirit? Are there any special preparations? All you have to do is read about the Holy Spirit in the Scriptures to acquaint yourself; and ask for it in prayer.

By the account of Job 22:21, if you acquaint yourself with God, and make peace with Him by the blood of Jesus; God's goodness will come upon you.

And as you desire the baptism of the Holy Spirit, you will receive it as ministers pray over you (Acts 8:14-17; 19:5-6).

Indwelling Spirit and the outpouring of the Holy Spirit are both separate spiritual experiences, and are both rights of every believer.

Gal. 4:6

> **6 And because you are sons, God has sent forth the Spirit of His Son into your hearts, crying out, "Abba, Father!"**

The Holy Spirit has come since the day of Pentecost. What is left now is for believers to receive Him. Have you?

CHAPTER 9

Peace and Joy

Peace of life, peace of mind, peace of the body and joy is God's desire and plan for man. God envisaged His man Adam to dwell in total peace. It was not God's design that man be assailed and assaulted, and defeated by elements, forces and circumstances of life. Perfect peace was His original plan for man.

Peace, by definition means absence of war, trouble and troubling circumstances. But peace also means calmness of mind in face of troubles or troubling situations.

God showed clearly in His Word what His plan is for His creature man regarding peace.

Isa. 26:3

> **3 You will keep him in perfect peace, whose mind is stayed on You, because he trusts in You.**

Isa. 48:18

> **18 Oh, that you had heeded My commandments! Then your peace would have been like a river, and your righteousness like the waves of the sea.**

Isa 54:10

> **10 For the mountains shall depart and the hills be removed, but My kindness shall not depart from you, nor shall My covenant of peace be removed, "says the Lord, who has mercy on you.**

To enjoy the best of the land in the atmosphere of perfect peace, covenanted peace like a river, is God's great plan for believers. Perfect peace is possible, and that is God's goal for man. Walking with God, you can attain it.

Covenant of Peace

God says, He will give man covenant of peace. How can one enter into this promised peace?

First, note the Bible says there is no peace for a wicked man (Isa. 48:22). A wicked man is a sinner – a man who walks contrary to God. The Bible calls him a son of disobedience (Eph. 2:2).

To enter this arena of perfect peace, a man must first make peace with God because sin puts man on a war path with God. Sin makes man an outright enemy of God. Can you receive a man's good with who you are in enmity?

A sinner is one who is a friend of the world; one who loves the world more than God; one who disobeys God. Disobedience is rebellion; the Bible calls it witchcraft (1 Sam 15:23). No one who belongs to this class can enjoy the peace of God.

The children of Israel at the time of Judges enjoyed perfect peace when they gave themselves up to obeying God's commandments. The moment they began to stray and disobey God's injunctions, their peace was withdrawn. They entered into crisis of servitude and domination by foreign nations. Until they repented and cried out to God in repentance, then God relents and restored their peace and independence.

For a man to enter into this enduring peace of God, he must make peace with God, by the blood of the cross. That is, he must repent of his sins, be washed in the blood of the Lamb (that is, be born again) - Rom. 5:1-2.

It's the grace of salvation upon which we stand as believers (Titus 2:11);and it was made possible by the sacrifice of Christ's blood on the cross.

What does it mean to make peace with God? It means to quit being an enemy of God; to stop being a son of disobedience. For the Bible says there can never be peace for a sinner (Isa. 52:22).

To make peace with God means to repent of your sins and be born again – accept Jesus Christ as Lord and Savior. The Bible says Jesus Christ is our peace (Eph. 2:14). Therefore, if you have Jesus you have peace. If you don't have Jesus, you can't have peace, and will never enjoy the covenant peace of God.

For the peace of God that surpasses all understanding to rest upon you, you must first make peace with God. On our own, we couldn't make peace with God, being sinners (outcast from the kingdom of God). Jesus Christ stood in the gap, as it were, and paid for our peace with the blood of the cross – His own blood shed at Calvary. That's why Jesus Christ is our peace. God's irrevocable promise to believers is His peace (Ps. 39:37).

Worry – Thief of Peace

Every believer has a right to God's peace. Peace is the covenant right of a believer. Yet you will be surprised that a lot of believers are peace-less. Many are full of anxieties and worries, which rob them of peace. I ascribe this to ignorance.

The Bible says, God speaking, my people are destroyed for lack of knowledge (Hosea 4:6). As a believer, if you acquaint yourself thoroughly with Word of God, you will be able to claim successfully the promise pf peace.

God has promised believers His perfect peace. He pledged that His peace will guide our minds and hearts through Jesus Christ (verse 7). But there is a condition to fulfill: fret not and worry not; be prayerful and be thankful.

When you as a believer do that first part, you will certainly realize the second part (the promise of peace).

Total peace of life is God's design for His children. It's not God's desire that a believer be consumed by the worries and cares of life. Cares and worries are burdens God never intended for a believer to bear. That's why the Bible says in the epistle of Peter, to cast all your cares on the Lord.

God wants you to have His perfect peace rather than be worry-ridden and afflicted.

I am reminded of a case of a sister who came to a man of God for prayer. Her prayer request was that God should lessen her burden of cares.

God says to hand over your total load of cares (all not a portion) to Him. But some would rather, God takes just part of it.

Sometimes, ignorance is the undoing of many Christians. God assuredly wants to carry 100% of my cares, and give me all His rest. Why would I want to give Him only half of it? If you have this understanding as a believer, you sure will have abundant peace.

Knowledge is power. If you are acquainted with the Word of God you will be strong.

Peace in Kinds

Before we end this segment, it is necessary to state that there are two kinds of peace – the peace of God and the peace of the world. The two are diametrically opposed.

Peace, from the world perspective, is absence of war or trouble or violence. Such peace is often fragile, ephemeral, short-lived and undependable.

On the other hand, the peace of God is longer-lasting, transparent and dependable. Peace of God is not necessarily absence of trouble but a restful mind that is encapsulated with assurances of God's presence and power that overrides all problems. Know that with God all things are possible. And the fact that our battle belongs to God, makes a believer more than a conqueror.

It's a solid rock peace – ways above worldly peace. It's unique; it's perfect and unfailing. Hear Jesus talk about this peace in the gospel of John.

John 14:27

> **27 Peace I leave with you, My peace I give to you; not as the world gives do I give to you. Let not your heart be troubled, neither let it be afraid.**

Peace in God's way and style; God's own peace is the right of every believer. This does not mean absence of storms of life. Of course, there will be storms; for Jesus said in the world believers will have tribulation (storms). But even in those storms, believers have a promise of God's peace because Christ has overcome the world (represented by those storms). Jesus' victory is believer's victory.

God's peace is the right of believers. God desires and plans that His children dwell in perfect peace, untroubled by circumstances and elements of the world.

Are you a believer? Where have you been searching for peace? Peace like a river is God's promise for you. Only trust and believe in Him – let your mind rest continually on Him (not fretting, not worrying) and you will enjoy His covenant of peace.

Believer's Right to Joy

Another exciting right of a believer is joy. As we said earlier, the moment a sinner repents and receives the new birth (that is, born again), he receives instantly the indwelling Holy Spirit. This enables him to bear divine fruits.

Remember as we said earlier, there are nine divine '*fruits*' of the spirit. The Bible list them as love, joy, peace, longsuffering, kindness, goodness, faithfulness, gentleness and self-control (Gal 5:22-23).

These fruits are to manifest routinely in a believer's life because of the presence of Holy Spirit. One can say that joy, peace, love etc. are believer's 'second' nature (the overriding nature that has come to override the nature of sin from which he is delivered).

A believer ought to be known by these heavenly traits. This is the ideal – that does not in any way suggest that it's idealistic, far-fetched or unrealizable. No! It's God's design, and it's practical and 'practice-able'.

'
.

Of course, we know that in the body of Christ the reverse may be the case. Don't blame God for this – He has made the needed provisions for us to live and manifest the fruit of the Spirit.

In First Corinthians 3:22 the Bible says *all things are yours.*

If the testimony you are witnessing is contrary to what we are saying, put the blame on the believers who have failed to acquaint themselves with the Word of God and live up to God demands and provisions for their lives. You can claim every promise of God in His Word and it will work for you; if only you know them or that such exist.

God's power has given to us everything we need to live a holy and successful life. Every need of our lives has been spiritually provided for in abundance in the Word of God.

It's written, that God's divine power has given to us all things concerning life; and all things required to make life and living sweet (2 Peter 1:3); and that we, as believers, are beneficiaries of all spiritual blessings (Eph. 1:3). That power that gave us all things is Christ; the platform that made us possessors of all blessings is Christ's death and resurrection. These I consider the riches of His mercy and grace.

If you are not realizing these blessings, check your life. Be sure you are not living in sin; be sure you are not walking by sight (instead of by faith); be sure you have not been fretting and worrying, walking in doubt and unbelief.

You cannot claim the promises of the Bible except you come to God according to His Word (Mark 11:24; 1 John 5:14-15), and with faith in His Word.

All our needs are provided for in the Word of God. To put it better, every need of a believer is provided and paid for by the blood of Jesus Christ (Heb. 8:6; 9:15). His blood is the seal of our covenant.

But you must walk by faith and not by sight to avail yourself of these promises (2 Cor. 5:7). Believe what God says in His Word concerning you. Learn to confess continually God's promises for your life. Confession creates reality.

Believe this! It's your Father's pleasure to bless you with peace and joy. God does not intend His children to be consumed by adverse circumstances and sorrow. That's why believers are vessels of mercy and not of wrath (Rom. 9:22-23). This also accounts for the reason for repeated warning not to worry nor fret (Phil. 4:6), and to cast your whole cares upon God (1 Pet 5:7; Ps. 55:22).

Believers are surrounded and encapsulated by God's mercies, so that they be preserved and empowered to enjoy life (Lam 3:22-23).

God's designs are that a believer dwells in fullness of joy. Check it out. The provisions are in His Word.

When we ask and receive, and He supplies all our needs beyond our asking or imagination, would we not dwell in fullness? We know this to be true because God cannot lie (Num. 23:19, Titus 1:2) and his Word does not fail (Ps. 33:8-9; 119:89; 138:2; Isa. 55:10-11).

2 Cor. 1:20-22

20 For all the promises of God in Him are Yes, and in Him Amen, to the glory of God through us.

21 Now He who establishes us with you in Christ and has anointed us is God,

22 who also has sealed us and given us the Spirit in our hearts as a guarantee.

Believe it, it's your Father's delight to give you the kingdom (Luke 12:32). Peace and joy are believer's covenant rights.

On a final note, we say here that, not to live in joy is to reject God's best for your life; it is to displease Him. To displease God is to sin. Why? God commands us variously to rejoice (Phil 4:4, 1 Thess. 5:16-17).

Anyone who goes through life sorrowing and complaining is walking in unbelief and doubt. Unbelief and doubting is sin. To doubt God is sin. The Bible says without faith we cannot receive from God.

God commands believers to rejoice. And rejoice you must because God is able to do all things (Jer. 32:27; Luke 1:37). He is God who makes the impossibilities of our lives possible; who reverses the irreversible.

God is He who gives us His ALL (Jesus Christ); would He not with Him freely give us all things (Rom. 8:32). I am persuaded He will. There is, absolutely, nothing that is too hard for God.

Let your song be the glorious song of Habakkuk.

Hab. 3:17-18

> **17 Though the fig tree may not blossom, nor fruit be on the vines; though the labor of the olive may fail, and the fields yield no food; though the flock may be cut off from the fold, and there be no herd in the stalls —**
>
> **18 Yet I will rejoice in the Lord, I will joy in the God of my salvation.**

The believer has right to be joyful. It is our strength in the body of Christ.

To key effectively into this commandment and divine provision for joy and rejoicing, you need daily renewal by the Holy Spirit. You achieve this through daily fellowship with God in Word and prayer/praise.

As you continually receive the infilling of Holy Spirit you will bear the fruit of joy and peace and love in your life.

Paul confirmed that joy and peace are believers' rightful inheritances, when he prayed for the Romans, that the God of hope would fill them with joy and peace in their knowledge of, and association with Christ, so that, by the power of the Holy Spirit, they would abound in hope. Rom 15:13

Joy and peace belong to believers. And I say to you believer, keep your joy and peace; watch and guard them against satanic attack. How? By doing what the Lord commands in Philippians chapter four: show no anxiety in any situation, but take all things to God in prayer with believing thanksgiving (Phil 4:6-7).

Fretting, worrying, doubting will steal, kill, and destroy your joy and peace. Give no place to the devil. Follow Habakkuk in his hymn of joy, and receive the anointing of gladness above all your fellows.

CHAPTER 10

Divine Access

Divine access is one of the wonderful rights and privileges of believers. A believer has access to God not just in one way but in several great ways. As believers, our access to God is full and unlimited.

In Old Testament time, the children of Israel did not have full access to God. At best, their access was partial, limited and restricted. First, their leaders as we had shown earlier (the prophets, the priests and the kings) were their guide and mediators.

God spoke to the people through their appointed leaders. The people did not have and could not enjoy personal direction and guidance of the Holy Spirit (cf. Rom. 8:14).

Besides, the people depended on their leaders for prayers and offerings (remember the regulations and institution in Leviticus for diverse offerings or burnt sacrifice). They depended on the priests. They did not have nor exercised direct access to God.

That was the dispensation of the Old Testament. But all that came to an end in one day, when Jesus Christ expired on the cross and the veil of the temple was torn from the top to the bottom. This, Bible scholars believe, signaled the end of the old order, as it were (Matt 27:45-53).

The death and resurrection of Jesus Christ started, and established the New Testament dispensation (New Covenant). Jesus' blood was the surety for the new covenant (Heb. 8:6).

Under the Old Testament, the nation of Israel comprised the children of Jacob, who was a servant of God. But under the New Covenant, believers in Christ are children of God (not servants).

Gal. 4:4-7

> **4 But when the time had fully come, God sent his Son, born of a woman, born under law,**
>
> **5 to redeem those under law, that we might receive the full rights of sons.**
>
> **6 Because you are sons, God sent the Spirit of his Son into our hearts, the Spirit who calls out, "Abba, Father."**
>
> **7 So you are no longer a slave, but a son; and since you are a son, God has made you also an heir.**

The Bible says as many as received Jesus and believed in Him were granted the right to be children of God. The above Scripture says believers are granted the privilege to *receive the full rights of sons.* It's an act of great love and grace.

The first of epistle of John invites believers to consider what manner of love God has bestowed on them in making them His children (1 John 3:1-2).

Believers are children of God, and as children we have every access to God the Father as any son would have of his father – unlimited, total, full and unrestricted. Let's look at just three aspects of this divine access.

Eternal Life

Eternal or everlasting life is God-kind of life or better still, it's God's life; divine life from heaven. No one had this access until Christ went to the cross and rose from the dead. Adam almost gate-crashed into it but he was prevented.

When Adam was created, he was made in the image of God, holy and righteous. He had a choice between two parallel destinies: taking the tree of life and live forever or taking the fruit of the tree of knowledge of good and evil. He chose the latter against the will of God, and he became defiled and lost his holy identity.

And to ensure he did not eat the tree of life and live forever, God drove him out of the Garden of Eden. (Gen. 3:22-24)

If Adam had laid his hand on the tree of life, He would have caught the eternal life. But God made sure he did not have that access when he committed sin.

Of the generations of the old dispensation, none had eternal life. They all died – the righteous to rise at rapture to life (eternal life), while the unrighteous would rise at judgment time for judgment. But the stock of the new dispensation (New Testament), the righteous like Peter and Paul and the others, all slept in the Lord (they did not die because they had received eternal life). Jesus said he who believes in Him shall not die (John 11:25).

The tree of life has that principle or essence called eternal (everlasting) life. It was meant for Adam to eat and live forever. But when he disobeyed God, the access to the tree of life was denied and withdrawn.

Eternal life came with the New Testament – it's a divine product of the new covenant. Only believers in Christ who have received the new birth (that is, are born again) have eternal life. Unbelievers don't have it. It is the right of a Christian only (John 3:15-16).

1 John 5:11-12

> **11 And this is the testimony: that God has given us eternal life, and this life is in His Son.**
>
> **12 He who has the Son has life; he who does not have the Son of God does not have life.**

The one who has the son is a reference to believers – those who are born again. He who does not have the son refers to an unbeliever.

An unbeliever can't have eternal life – all he has is the wrath of God. That's why the Bible aptly labels them as vessels of wrath programmed for destruction (Rom. 9:21-23).

A believer has free, full access to divine life (eternal life). One interesting and refreshing thing about eternal life in believers is that it cannot perish. What does that mean? A believer does not die. It may sound shocking and unbelievable, but it's true. Jesus says so in the gospel of John chapter eleven (John 11:25-26).

Believers don't die; they just sleep at the time of their departure, to wake up in heaven above. It's a translocation, and not death (1 Cor. 15:6, 51).

Do you believe this? I do! God cannot lie. After rapture, at the end of it all, believers will have access to the tree of life that was denied Adam (Rev. 22:2).

Heaven Citizenship

Heaven citizenship is another right of a believer. If God is our Father (and indeed He is), His home is our abode as His children (believers in Christ). Heaven is where God's throne is – His abode (Isa. 66:1). And heaven is the home of every believer.

Prior to His departure from the earth, Jesus told His disciples that He was returning to the Father to prepare mansions for them.

Jesus said, before going to the Cross, that He was going ahead of believers to prepare mansions for them in heaven (John 14:1-3).

Yes, mansions in heaven! Each believer has one of those awaiting him.

We may not know now the shape and size of these mansions, but I am persuaded to believe there are, because Jesus Christ says so. And He will come back soon to take believers home, because as He says, where He is now (heaven) is where believers will also be. That proves that heaven is believers' eternal abode.

Believers will not enter heaven in flesh and blood, that is, as we are now. In a twinkle of an eye at the sound of the trumpet, according to the revelation given to Paul, we shall be transformed: mortal earthly bodies will assume immortal, glorious, celestial bodies (1 Cor. 15:50-53).

The above Scriptures are saying that believers shall inherit the kingdom of heaven but not with this mortal, corruptible body (flesh and blood).

At the time of translocation, believers will assume spiritual, celestial, glorious bodies, like Christ resurrection body. This shows that heaven's citizenship is a reality believers have right to, and will enjoy in time to come.

Jesus Christ is the way to that glorious abode. Walk with Him and you will not miss your way. Believers have right to heaven, it's their Father' home.

Apostle Paul caught this revelation some time in his ministry when he described a believer as a citizen of heaven. This is the kingdom believers will possess at the time of rapture, when Jesus will change their mortal bodies into glorious bodies like His own (Phil. 3:20-21).

And this iswhat Paul saw toward the end of his ministry on earth; a man who was done with his work, and saw with the eyes of faith the crown, and heavenly abode beckoning on him.

Paul's revelation in 2 Timothy 4:5-8, is both a warning and an encouragement to Timothy, as well as a consolation and rejoicing for Paul, who had kept the faith to the end and was about to be crowned. Hallelujah!

This was also the same encouragement and comforting Jesus gave to His disciples about the time of His departure. It was a needed tonic and motivation for the disciples, who were soon to be bereaved (by Jesus' death), and the challenges of Jewish hostilities waiting in the wings for them.

Jesus Christ said repeatedly to His disciples, you are not of the world just as I am not of the world (John15:18-19). If they were not 'citizens' of the world (that is, not of the world), then what citizens are they? Of heaven, of course.

When we assert that a believer has a right to heavenly citizenship, we mean it as a matter of fact or truth, so to speak.

The moment a sinner repents and gives his life to Christ, he has Christ's guarantee of his heavenly citizenship. The blood of Jesus is our seal – our guarantee. But a believer has duty to guard his salvation (and associated blessings or rights) jealously, and also work it out. How?

He has to determine to follow Christ, not turning to the left or right (backsliding) but walking continually on the path of righteousness. If you hold onto the end like Paul, you can rest assured that you have heaven.

There is a working out to do. A believer must work out his salvation. Though our spirit is regenerated (born again), our soul and flesh are not born again (Jas. 2:21). There are areas of continual temptation in our lives – the flesh, the world, and Satan.

We have instant salvation at the point of being born again. Thereafter, we need to maintain our watch, and keep our salvation current (progressive salvation) by faith, obedience and works of righteousness. This will deliver the ultimate salvation, like Paul says in the epistle to the Philippians.

Phil 1:19-20 KJV

> **19 For I know that this shall turn to my salvation through your prayer, and the supply of the Spirit of Jesus Christ,**

However, some believe in the dogma of eternal security: once saved always saved. In other words, they claim that once a person is saved, even if along the way he commits fornication and backslides (not repenting), he will still make heaven. That is the doctrine of the demons; not the doctrine of our Lord Jesus Christ.

I consider that as a veritable license to sin; is it not like a dog going back to its vomit? God forbid!

Every believer needs to work out his salvation (that is, maintain on-going or progressive salvation), in order to cap it with ultimate salvation.

Like we say in the world of business, an enterprise is either an on-going concern or a liquidated one. A sinner or a backslider is a liquidated entity, but a believer must remain an on-going concern (that is, maintaining progressive salvation).

Note that the Bible calls believers the righteousness of God in Christ (2 Cor. 5:21), and holy (Col. 3:12; 1 Pet. 2:9). That righteousness and holiness, you must maintain to get to heaven.

But, righteousness is a gift of God to every believer (Ps. 24:5; Rom. 5:17). We cannot be righteous on own account – a man's self-righteousness is as a filthy rag (Isa. 64:6). It's the redeeming blood of Jesus Christ that confers God's righteousness on a believer, because God justifies him on the account of his faith in Christ (Rom. 5:1).

Of course, two cannot walk together if there is no agreement. So, if a believer sins and will not repent (that is, he is backslidden), he goes out of fellowship with God because of Amos 3:3. He loses his cloak of righteousness and garment of salvation. He is hell-bound.

One who backslides loses his *garment of salvation* and *robe of righteousness*. That is the story of a believer who backslides.

A backslider is one who sins but refuses to repent and be restored, but keeps rather multiplying sin (Matt. 18:15-17; Gal. 6:1). Such one falls out of agreement and fellowship with the Lord.

The doctrine of eternal security is a falsehood – a deception of Satan. Nonetheless, a believer has right to heavenly citizenship.

Access to God

In the New Covenant era, unlike the Old Testament time, believers have direct and immediate access to God. The leave was granted the moment Christ, hanging on the cross, cried out and expired, having breathed His last (Matt. 27:50-51).

Significantly, the veil of the temple was torn in two from the top to the bottom. This was the token of the permission or access granted to believers. From there, believers now have direct access to God, never again to depend on priest or high priest or any other intermediary. Our faith in Christ gave us the access, because He is the Way.

Before then, access to the presence of God (the Holy of Holies) was kept barred from all except the High Priest, who enters there once in a year during the Jewish ceremony of National Atonement.

But beginning from Jesus' sacrificial death on the cross, believers have unrestricted access to God. That's why Paul assertively could say, come boldly to the throne of grace (God's presence) and get help (Heb. 4:16**.**).

Here, we have an open invitation to approach His Majesty, to court for mercy so that favor (help) may flow to us.

This underscores the fact that the key to God's favor or help is mercy (Ps. 102:13). Mercy is what singles a man out for divine visitation or miracle or breakthrough. A believer needs to court the mercy of God continually, that the light of God's countenance may shine on him.

The interesting thing about the New Covenant dispensation is that, a believer no longer needs an intermediary like prophets or priests to connect God. Such guides have been done away with.

The believer now has the Holy Spirit. He alone is the One who leads and guides the believer.

This is the primary way (number one way) God guides believers –the indwelling Holy Spirit. God instructs and teaches us through the Holy Spirit (not through any prophet or priest as of the Old Testament era).

The Holy Spirit is given as believer's teacher, Guide, Helper, Comforter, and Advocate. He is our Guide forever says Ps 48:14.

To a believer, this psalm is a reference to the Holy Spirit; He is the One who will be with us till the end.

Another Biblical truth that underpins and establishes believer's access to God is Christ instruction regarding prayer in the New Testament era. He out-rightly gave us the permission to ask God the Father in His name, whatever we are in need of. Go to the Father in my name, He said.

A believer has the right to go to the Father in the name and authority of Jesus. Jesus, before His death, granted us this leave or permission (John 16:23-24). He said categorically, go to the Father in my name over any issue or need.

This leave was granted only under the New Covenant. It's the hallmark of believer's unmitigated access to the throne of grace (God's presence).

Believer – you sure have access! Take advantage of it! Make good use of it.

Privilege of Prayer

The privilege of prayer is yet another sub-set of divine access. Any discussion on divine access without mention of prayer is incomplete.

Prayer is a significant sign-post or hallmark of our relationship with our Creator.

Prayer is a religious activity, and a spiritual exercise. It's religious because it's clothed with worship and devotion. And at the same time it's spiritual in essence, being an activity that seeks to engage or contact the supernatural.

What is prayer? One definition says prayer is the act or privilege of communicating with God. When we pray, we seek to enter into communication with the Supernatural Being, God.

Prayer is an active rather than passive communication. It's a dialogue with God, not a monologue, as it appears to some people. That it is a dialogue is what makes it an active exercise (and not passive, like a monologue). It's active because you are speaking to, and with a supernatural Being, who hears and answers.

Jer. 33:3

> **3 'Call to Me, and I will answer you, and show you great and mighty things, which you do not know.'**

Believers ought to have confidence in God that He will answer prayers and supply every need of believers, that are in accordance with His will (1 John 5:14-15).

Of truth, God hears, and answers prayers.

Prayer is communication indeed – a means of sending and receiving information or help. God ordained prayer as a channel of communication between Him and His people. This communication, as we have said, is clothed in worship, which makes it essentially a fellowship and communion. This is rightly the privilege of God's people.

For sake of emphasis, I say only God's people? Yes! Because the Bible says so severally.

Prov. 15:26

26 The thoughts of the wicked are an abomination to the Lord, But the words of the pure are pleasant.

Prov. 15:8-9

8 The sacrifice of the wicked is an abomination to the Lord, but the prayer of the upright is His delight.

9 The way of the wicked is an abomination to the Lord, but He loves him who follows righteousness.

The wicked means the sinner or unbeliever. The ways or thoughts of a sinner are an abomination to God (that is, detestable). Thoughts lead to words; and words represent thoughts; and words represent prayer.

Likewise, prayer represents sacrifice because it involves giving of yourself, loyalty, allegiance and love to the object of your worship.

Prayer is not for the wicked; it's not meant for a sinner (unbeliever). The Bible confirms this further in Prov. 1:28 and Isa 59:1-2:

The wicked, the sinner, the unbeliever is separated from God. He will not be heard. In fact, the Psalmist says God is angry with the sinner every day (Ps. 7:11).

Prayer is ordained by God – as a divine medium He instituted to give currency to His relationship with His people (believers in Christ). It's a holy way believers service and keep alive their union with God in Trinity.

Prayer is God's invitation to His people to engage Him in holy dialogue. God created man for worship and fellowship (Gen. 3:8). Prayer is one of the media through which this divine purpose is served and fulfilled.

Why should believers pray? What is the motive of believers' prayer? Believers pray because it helps them to sustain and maintain living relationship and fellowship with God.

Prayer is the privilege of believers alone – it's both the delight of a believer as much as it's the delight of God. God covets it because the Bible says He longs for our worship (John 4:23).

The book of Isaiah recorded a scene where God was expressing His displeasure at Israel, who refused to seek His fellowship and counsel but went up to Egypt instead to seek help (Isa. 30:1-3).

Another reason why believers must pray is that God does not do anything on earth except in answer to prayer. The ruler of the world is Satan because Adam sold out his authority to him at the Garden of Eden. Therefore, God will not interfere on the earth except at believers' invitation (prayer). The world currently is another man's territory - Satan's. Believers do not belong to the world, as we said earlier. God can't interfere yet unless the believers invite Him to. That's why you must ask – God Himself demands that we ask.

How should a believer pray? A believer can pray with understanding or in the spirit. Praying with understanding is praying out of the mind (or soul) in a known language. Praying in the spirit is praying out of your heart (spirit) in unknown utterance (praying in tongues).

1 Cor. 14:14-15

> **14 For if I pray in a tongue, my spirit prays, but my understanding is unfruitful.**
>
> **15 What is the conclusion then? I will pray with the spirit, and I will also pray with the understanding. I will sing with the spirit, and I will also sing with the understanding.**

Praying in other tongues is a privilege of only the believers. The Bible says he who prays in an unknown tongue speaks mysteries to God. And because he has the help and support of the Holy Spirit, he prays in the perfect will of God (Rom. 8:26-27).

What a great privilege believers have in prayer! To underscore this point, God says to His beloved (believers) severally, *"Ask"* - Matt 7:7-8; John 15:7

When it comes to the matter of prayer, the following Scriptures are very reassuring.

John 16:23-24

> **23** **"And in that day you will ask Me nothing. Most assuredly, I say to you, whatever you ask the Father in My name He will give you.**

> **24** **Until now you have asked nothing in My name. Ask, and you will receive, that your joy may be full.**

Are you a believer? Prayer is your right, privilege and a special possession. God seeks it (John 4:23; Jer. 33:3; 29:11-13); in all the ways the Scriptures prescribed – with understanding, in tongues, in songs and psalms and praise (Eph. 5:18, 19).

Through prayer and worship, God seeks to answer you; bless you and make your joy overflow. Take full advantage of this opportunity, and privilege of prayer.

CHAPTER 11

Spiritual Authority in Christ

T he discussion on believer's rights and privileges will be incomplete without a mention of spiritual authority of believers in Christ. This is an area that is new to many Christians, and has been much less explored, and much less exploited.

Do believers have any authority in Christ? Do believers have power over Satan and demons? Are demons subject to a believer? Can a believer exercise authority over Satan? I say yes, yes, yes!

Turning the Pyramid Upside Down

From the beginning of creation, Adam was next to Godhead in hierarchy, and Satan was under him. Adam was on top of God's creation, ruling over all God's works on earth. Adam was practically the god of the earth (Ps. 8:1-6).

But the day Adam yielded to Satan, and disobeyed God, the pyramid was turned upside down. How? Satan took over as the god of the earth, and Adam became subject to Satan as a consequence. Adam and all his descendants came under Satan's authority and manipulation.

The Battle of the Cross

The cross of Jesus Christ (upon which He died) was an instrument of both shame and curse, at the beginning (Gal. 3:13). But when Jesus Christ rose from the dead, the cross became a symbol of power and glory.

Jesus Christ rose triumphantly from the dead, and took the keys of death and hell from Satan; and recovered the authority Satan stole and usurped from Adam.

Col 2:14-15

> **14 having wiped out the handwriting of requirements that was against us, which was contrary to us. And He has taken it out of the way, having nailed it to the cross.**
>
> **15 Having disarmed principalities and powers, He made a public spectacle of them, triumphing over them in it.**

Rev 1:18

> **18 I am He who lives, and was dead, and behold, I am alive forevermore. Amen. And I have the keys of Hades and of Death.**

Jesus Christ through His death and resurrection delivered us from the authority and power of Satan. Those who will come to believe in Christ will no more be subject to Satan, but have become empowered to exercise authority over him.

Yes, believers have authority over Satan. Believers have been delivered from the power of Satan and his dark kingdom (Col 1:12-14).

Christ Investment of Power on Believer

When Jesus was raised from the dead, He received ALL authority and power that were in all the three realms – heaven, earth and under the earth.

Matt 28:18-19

> **18 And Jesus came and spoke to them, saying, "All authority has been given to Me in heaven and on earth.**
>
> **19 Go therefore and make disciples of all the nations, baptizing them in the name of the Father and of the Son and of the Holy Spirit,**

All authority in heaven and earth has been given to me,' Jesus declared triumphantly. Likewise, the Psalmist declared prophetically, that all power belong to God (Ps 62:11).

Jesus recovered the power Satan usurped, and immediately delegated it to the church, when He said, *'therefore, go'.* Believers by this are commanded to go with the authority of Christ, and exercise the authority on earth over Satan and demons, and over situations of life. And this we do by speaking the word of faith (God's Word) and believing it for its manifestation.

There's no doubt that believers do have authority over Satan and his cohorts. Hear what Christ said to the 72 disciples who had gone out on an assignment.

Luke 10:19

> **19 Behold, I give you the authority to trample on serpents and scorpions, and over all the power of the enemy, and nothing shall by any means hurt you.**

Authority and power to trample upon serpents and scorpions. These are reverences to Satan and demons – they are the enemies of believers. Believers are given authority over all the powers of the enemy.

Do believers have spiritual authority over Satan? Yes! This next Scripture proves it further.

Jesus says in Mark 16:16-18 that certain miraculous signs will follow those who believe in Him. The first sign: *believers shall cast out demons.* We can't cast out demons except we have authority over them. Can we?

That we can cast out the devils means explicitly that we have authority over them in the name of Jesus Christ.

The second sign the Bible says is *that believers will lay hands upon the sick and they shall recover.* Sickness and disease are oppressions of Satan (Acts 10:38). And if believers can heal the sick in the name of Jesus (overcoming Satan's evil work of sickness) then believers do have power or authority over the enemy called Satan.

To see how powerful a believer is in Christ, the Bible says even the aprons and handkerchief from the body of Paul healed sickness and cast out demons (Acts 19:11-12).

I heard a story some time ago about a man of God, to whom a mad man was brought. The pastor merely said, *come out of him in the name of Jesus*, and the mad man became instantly healed.

Jesus Christ confirmed it that believers have God-given authority on earth; and real spiritual authority over Satan, and demons. He did that also in the following Scripture.

Matt 18:18

> **18 "Assuredly, I say to you, whatever you bind on earth will be bound in heaven, and whatever you loose on earth will be loosed in heaven.**

Whatever a believer binds here on earth, God upholds in heaven. Believers are given power to bind the works of the enemy or to loose them with heaven's backing and approval.

Whatever you bind, according to some other versions, means whatever you forbid and declare improper or unlawful.

Some Bible scholars believe this text is about discipline in the church – regarding admission to and rejection from membership of the church.

But some of us believe that this text has a secondary application. Whatever things you forbid and declare to be improper or unlawful will be upheld by heaven. And whatever things you permit and declare to be proper or lawful will receive heaven's backing.

This text certainly does have wider application. For instance, sickness is an oppression of Satan. If you permit it, it will stay and abide with you. But if you forbid it and disallow it, and declare it to be an "unlawful possession or attachment" it will leave you.

To unbelievers, sickness will be a lawful attachment because they are subject to Satan and his evil works. But, to a believer your rightly possession and inheritance is divine health and perfect soundness. It's well within your ambit as a believer to disallow sickness and other evil works of Satan.

Believers have Christ-given authority to bind and to loose.

Arise and exercise your authority over Satan and demons.

This same authority to bind or loose; to forbid or permit was the authority I exercised in the year 2000 to receive divine health. You can do it, too.

Made Alive with Christ

The Scriptures give more insight on the dimensions of this authority of believers.

Eph. 2:1

And you He made alive, who were dead in trespasses and sins,

The Bible says, as sinners we were dead people (that is, spiritually). But God raised us up – He raised us up when He raised Jesus from the dead. Verse 5 says God made us alive together with Christ.

According to the Bible, we were not just raised up with Christ; we are prominently seated with Christ in glory (verse 6). Hallelujah!

How are believers seated? *In heavenly places in Christ Jesus.* In other words, where Christ is seated now is where a believer is seated.

We need to get a better view and understanding of our authority in Christ. And we see that in the next Scriptures.

Eph. 1:19-23

19 and what is the exceeding greatness of His power toward us who believe, according to the working of His mighty power

20 which He worked in Christ when He raised Him from the dead and seated Him at His right hand in the heavenly places,

21 far above all principality and power and might and dominion, and every name that is named, not only in this age but also in that which is to come.

22 And He put all things under His feet, and gave Him to be head over all things to the church,

The Bible says the mighty power of God raised Jesus Christ from the dead and seated Him at God's right hand in the heavenly places (v.20). The right hand of the throne is a place of power and authority.

Jesus sits at the right hand of God. Not only that, God in that position places Him far above all powers that are named in heaven and earth (v. 21), *placing ALL things under Jesus' feet.* That's an awesome position – awesome authority,

Remember, the Bible says Jesus Christ is the Head of the church (Eph. 1:22); and believers (the church) are the body of Christ.

Christ is the Head and believers are the body. Can you separate the head of a man from his body? No!

What is the implication of the above? Wherever the head lies is where the body is found. Therefore, if the Head (Christ) is seated at the right hand of Divine Majesty above all power, with all things under His feet, there precisely is where the body (the church or believers) are seated too. You can't separate the head and its body. This describes perfectly the awesome position and authority believers occupy in Christ.

The church needs to learn this and get acquainted with this truth. We believers have great authority in Christ. Believers have authority they know little about, and scarcely exercise. The earlier believers realize this and wake up to exercise that power the better for them.

Jesus after His resurrection delegated His authority to the church. But unfortunately many believers are waiting for God to act over certain situations in life while God is waiting for them to do something. Beloved, nothing will ever happen until you move. Until you act out your authority, God will not move.

Responsibility to Act

Jesus arising from the dead, received all authority in heaven and on earth, and immediately delegated this authority to the church, the body of Christ – to the body of Christ collectively and individually. Upon every believer is deposited the authority of Christ. Christ's authority is the right and privilege of every believer. Believers, therefore, have responsibility to act – to exercise this authority on earth on behalf of Christ.

Jesus said the works that He did, believers will also do, and even greater works. With what power or authority, I ask? We will, with Christ's delegated authority, of course.

For believers to do the works Christ did – healing the sick, casting out devils, and doing wonders – requires power or authority. Believers have no such power on their own except that delegated to them by Christ.

The gospels and the epistles both gave adequate proofs to show that believers do have spiritual authority and the responsibility to exercise it as we saw in the foregoing passages.

Furthermore, below are more scriptural proofs.

James 4:7

> **7 Therefore submit to God. Resist the devil and he will flee from you.**

If a believer doesn't have the power or authority to set the devil on the run, the Word of God (the Bible) would not have asked him to do such thing. In a similar manner the epistle of Peter directs believers to exercise their authority.

Also in 1 Peter 5:8-9 believers are commanded to resist the devil in faith. This shows that you have the authority to put the devil in check or set him to run.

As we said earlier, sickness is an oppression of Satan. Jesus says believers (not Jesus Himself) will lay hands on the sick and they shall be healed. In other words, believers have the authority to drive away Satan and his afflicting elements (sickness and disease), and it will be so.

If believers have no such authority, they cannot withstand and nullify and cancel Satan's works (which they do in the name and authority of Christ).

Talking about exercising Christ's authority, I have seen many healed and delivered from oppressions of Satan. Thank God for His indescribable gift; thank God too, for believers' spiritual authority.

To walk in Christ-given authority, a believer must first get acquainted with the relevant Scriptures; wake up to it, and begin to exercise this in faith.

But concerning a believer, the New Testament says "**Yet in all these things we are more than conquerors through Him who loved us**." (Rom 8:37).

In Christ, a believer is not just a conqueror; he is more than a conqueror. In other words, in Christ we believers have all victory.

Our chief enemy, Satan, is a defeated foe. On our behalf, Christ defeated Satan through His death and resurrection (Col. 2:14-15). If only the church has this understanding – that a believer has all authority and all victory, there would be no more fear, no more worry and anxiety.

The Bible in Phil. 4:13, saysthat I can do all things through Christ, who is my ally.(As a believer, you have the authority of Christ to do ALL THINGS.

If God be for us who can be against us, the Bible declares (Rom. 8:31). The Almighty God is your Ally. Can anyone, any power prevail or withstand any man who is backed up by God? Was that not the reason God told Joshua, that no man would be able to stand before him all the days of his life; because he had the same backing that Moses had(Josh. 1:5).

Are you a true believer? You are more than a conqueror.

1 John 4:4

> **4 You are of God, little children, and have overcome them, because He who is in you is greater than he who is in the world.**

You are an overcomer. The exceeding power of God (the Holy Spirit) dwells in you. The excellent wisdom of God dwells in you, too. You are blessed with all spiritual blessings in the heavenly places (Eph. 1:3). You have Christ's authority and victory as a believer.

Understand this; believe it, and rise up in faith and exercise God-given authority. You have Heaven's backing on all fronts – the Hosts of heaven are on your side.

This authority is exercised through the Word of God. That's why you must embrace the believer's responsibility of spiritual growth by feeding consistently on the Word of faith.

What you know of the Word of God, and how much of it you have in the inside of you, determines what success you can command in area of spiritual authority. That's why Satan works relentlessly to keep the body of Christ ignorant of their rights and inheritances in Christ.

Christ's authority and victory cannot fall on your laps like ripe berries. No. You got to do something. Feed continually on the Word of God, and by that empower your inner man to dwell richly in Christ's authority. And begin to wield the sword of the spirit in faith to possess your possessions, and occupy the territory God has rightly given to you. You truly do have authority. Begin now to exercise it!

CHAPTER 12

Heavenly Citizenship

The riches of the glory of believers' inheritance in Christ is beyond what ordinary human mind can grasp. Is that not why the Bible says, that no eye has ever seen, nor has any ear ever heard, nor has any heart ever imagined the wondrous things which God has prepared for those who love Him. (1 Cor. 2:9).

What blessings and what provisions God has prepared and made for believers, and the dimensions of it all, we can't fully understand now until we meet God in glory. Believers are awesomely endowed, gifted and blessed – blessed beyond measure.

You are not of the World.

Jesus once said to His disciples, 'You are not of the world just I am not of the world'. I guess, not many understood Him. And it's true indeed, as He said. Believers are in the world but they don't belong to the world (John 15:18-19).

Believers are chosen out of the world; they don't belong to the world. Believers belong somewhere else.

Yes, the ruler of this world (and the world systems) is Satan (John 14:30; 2 Cor. 4:4). Satan rules over all the unbelievers, and the unbelieving world. And as the Bible says, he takes them captive to do his will (2 Tim. 2:26).

But, Satan does not rule over believers because they do not belong to the world; and Jesus Christ is their Lord and Master. You can't serve two masters, can you?

The Lord and Master of every believer is Jesus Christ. And believers though living in the world do not belong to the world.

Believers' Citizenship

If believers do not belong to the world, where then do they belong to? God has clearly defined believers' citizenship according to what is written in the Bible.

Eph. 2:19

19 Now, therefore, you are no longer strangers and foreigners, but fellow citizens with the saints and members of the household of God,

Believers are no longer strangers and foreigners to God and the kingdom of God. Unbelievers are strangers and foreigners to God and His kingdom. Believers are the bonafide citizens, and blood-qualified members of the household of God. Because believers are specially chosen out of the world to enjoy this right and privilege.

The Word of God calls believers *a chosen generation. God's own special people, a holy nation unto God*(1 Peter 2:9-12). These indeed are what believers are.

And to underscore the fact of believers' citizenship, God emphatically called believers, *sojourners and pilgrims* on the earth. Why? Because the world is not their own, and they don't belong to it.

Heaven citizenship is the right and privilege of every believer. Hallelujah! Honorable conduct and godly lifestyle are the hallmarks of heavenly citizenship (Gal. 5:22-23).

Our citizenship is in heaven, and we shall take full possession of it when Jesus at rapture *transforms our lowly body to conform to His glorious body.* As a believer, look forward eagerly to taking possession of your mansion in heaven when Christ comes back (John 14:1-3).

There is a mansion in heaven awaiting every believer. What an exciting prospect! What a wonder of joy! Let's begin now to rejoice at this great gift of grace and love.

By the exceeding riches of God's grace, believers in Christ are citizens of heaven. That same great grace has also accorded believers the right of *heir-ship.* Believers are heirs of God – joint heirs with Christ, to the riches of God.

Eph. 3:6

6 that the Gentiles should be fellow heirs, of the same body, and partakers of His promise in Christ through the gospel,

Confirmed, believers are fellow heirs with Christ (Rom. 8:16-17). You can't be an heir unless you are a son. And as the Bible says, a slave does not abide in the house, but the son does. Believers are members of the household of God as heaven citizens. And because believers are sons of God, they are as well heirs of God. That's our right and privilege in Christ. We're qualified and made partakers of God's promises in Christ – one of these precious promises is heavenly citizenship. Hallelujah!

CHAPTER 13

Epilogue

A believer has more rights and privileges than we have discussed here. The purpose of this book is not to list every right of a believer but to highlight the special standing of believers in Christ of God, and our enviable inheritances (the inheritance of the saints in the light, as the Bible qualifies it).

By the account of the Scriptures, believers have glorious inheritance in Christ, and these inheritances are uncountable.

Eph. 1:3

> **3 Blessed be the God and Father of our Lord Jesus Christ, who has blessed us with every spiritual blessing in the heavenly places in Christ,**

Believers are granted **every spiritual blessing in heavenly places;** another version says **all spiritual blessings.** You cannot name them all – in Christ a believer is exceedingly rich. The Bible calls it **glorious inheritance.**

Eph. 1:18

> **that you may know what is the hope of His calling, what are the riches of the glory of His inheritance in the saints,**

We believers are so greatly favored and endowed. First, the Scripture says we were *predestined to adoption as sons* (Eph. 1:5). Only sons are heirs – not servants; sons have inheritance.

Secondly, the Bible also said that by token of that predestination, we *have obtained an inheritance in Christ* (verse 11). To finally prove this prized possession of believers, the Bible says also, *having believed in Christ, we were sealed with the Holy Spirit of promise, who is the guarantee of our inheritance* (verses 13 and 14). Hallelujah!

But as a closing remark, it must be stated here that these rights and privileges are not automatic. You don't need to work for them per se, but you sure need to qualify for them to enjoy them.

The Bible says in Col. 1:12 that God has qualified us to partake of the inheritance of the saints. There is a qualification that is required. That's why it's conditional. In other words, there are conditions you must fulfill.

We have touched variously on the conditions in the preceding chapters. First, the Bible says if you are willing and obedient you will enjoy the best of the land (Isa. 1:19).

God cannot force any man to do anything. We have our independent freewill. Man was created a free moral agent. If you become willing, and submit to the lordship of Jesus Christ, you will possess the ear-marked divine inheritances. If otherwise, you are unwilling, you certainly will not partake of the Lord's bounty for His chosen people (believers).

Besides, as a believer you must sustain the currency of your fellowship with God; walk in the spirit; waiting always on the Lord; be a hearer and doer of the Word, keeping a holy and bridled tongue, and serving the pure and undefiled religion of the Father in the care of orphans and widows, while keeping yourself unspotted from the world (Jas. 1:22-27).

These are some of God's charges to us, His elect and beloved. Pleasing Him must be our foremost delight and pursuit (Matt. 6:33). This is how we keep our aspect of the covenant, which guarantees and secures complimentary divine affirmation and blessing.

Every believer has a part and a role to play in this matter. Each one of us has the ability and power of choice. Decide which way you want to go and take your pick.

One key factor that facilitates our possession of these rights and privileges is knowledge. As a believer, you must endeavor to know what is rightly yours – the things God in His Word has promised you. Ignorance of the Word and your rights will keep you in perpetual denial and deprivation.

Acquaint yourself with God's precious promises in the Word. And exercise your faith and claim them.

God in Christ has established these inheritances for you; they are waiting for your claim. All you need to do is make your claim in prayer with faith. God said, ask and it shall be given to you. You don't need any special preparation; you don't need any lawyer. Once you're in right standing with the Lord, make your claim in faith and you will receive your inheritance.

Remain blessed in the mighty name of Jesus Christ, our Lord and Savior.

CHAPTER 14

Believer's Responsibilities

In creation, there is a duality that is both divine and natural, and as well pervasive. When God created a male (or man), He also created a female (or woman).

As there is light, so also there is darkness. There is a rainy season, and there is a dry season; just as there is a believer and an unbeliever.

In the preceding chapters, we have discussed believer's rights and privileges, but there is also at the other end of the spectrum, believer's responsibilities.

What is a Responsibility?

A responsibility is

1. A duty or work that we must do,
2. An obligation, that is, something that we are obliged or required to do;
3. A liability for which we are held accountable;
4. A commitment, that is, something that is demanded of us or we are bound to do

Believers truly do have responsibilities – spiritual responsibilities (not relational, not secular). Therefore, believer's responsibilities are duties, work or obligation we must undertake or fulfill. Our relationship with God is not all about rewards, rights and privileges, but also of responsibilities, duties and obligations to be met.

Believers have several responsibilities to fulfill. In this last chapter, we shall be discussing seven major responsibilities of a believer as follows:

Appendix 1 - Holiness,
Appendix 2- Spiritual Growth,
Appendix 3 - Soul Winning,
Appendix 4 - Giving.
Appendix 5 – Faith Growth
Appendix 6 – Walking in Love
Appendix 7 - Prayer

Of course, with responsibility comes authority (or empowerment) to procure success or achieve result.

God by His abundant grace and inexhaustible provisions has given to every believer the crucial authority or empowerment. First, the Bible says, we have grace given in accordance with or to the measure of God's gifting in our lives (Eph. 4:7).

And the Scripture adds that believers are the favored ones, who have received the *gift of righteousness* and *abundance of grace* (Rom. 5:17).

Grace is God's enabling power, through which God works in us both to will and to do according to His good pleasure. As believers, we are more than able to deliver all the responsibilities demanded of our lives. It's, of course, by God's grace at work in our lives.

I love the John's gospel report about believers, where it says that we have drunk of the fullness that is in Christ (John 1:16-17).

You have the grace to do and be all that God has determined and set for your life, as a believer. So the Scriptures affirm. Therefore, stand on that grace.

APPENDIX 1

Holiness

What is holiness? Holiness is a spiritual responsibility of a believer. It can be described as:

- ✓ Separation from ALL sin and immoral living. In Gal. 5:19-21, the Bible classified sins as the works of the flesh;
- ✓ Purity of life and morals;
- ✓ Consecration to the same end in life that God is consecrated to; dedicated to the same objective or focus that God is dedicated to;
- ✓ Unblameable – being blameless (1 Thess. 3:13).

Why is Holiness a Believer's Responsibility?

1. *It's God's command or injunction to believers.* God is our Father as believers. Like father, like son, a parable says. Believers must be holy in all conduct, because their Father is holy (1 Peter 1:15-16).

   Holiness was God's demand for the children of Israel in Old Testament (Lev. 19:2; 11:44-45). God does not change. He is the same yesterday, today and forever (Mal. 3:6; Heb. 13:8). Holiness has always been God's prime demand for those who will follow and walk after Him. It's an unchangeable rule or demand from the unchangeable God: *be holy, as I am holy.* Holiness is God's own very nature and identity. If you're living and practicing holiness, then the Holy God is your Father, and you are His son. But if you're not living holy, then God does not know you; and you're a bastard, not a son.

2. *Holiness is God's will for believers.* In other words, it's God's desire, choice, intention, decision and design, that believers live holy lives, and be holy in all manner of conversation. That's what it means to be made in the holy image of God.

   Paul's epistle *in 1 Thess. 4:3-5* says Our sanctification, that is, holiness, is God's choice; that we abstain from all uncleanness, is God's design. That's why God continually *works in us both to make us willing and able to do His good pleasure (*His choice, will, decision and design).

   According to Zechariah's prophecy in the gospel of Luke, believers are the people who are delivered from the hand of the enemy (Satan), to live without fear, but in holiness and righteousness (Luke 1:73-75).

3. *The first Adam was created in holiness and true righteousness.* God is holy and righteous (Lev. 19:2; Ps. 30:4; Isa. 6:3; 48:17). When God made the first man Adam, He created him in His image after His likeness. Thus, Adam was truly holy and righteous in his days of innocence, before the fall.

   Adam had the personal responsibility, duty and obligation to maintain that holiness. God was not to do it for him. But he failed and fell off from his own steadfastness (2 Pet. 3:17). Adam lost his rank, and became defiled and sin-ruined. As a result, sin and death began to rule over mankind (Rom. 5:12).

But the last Adam, Jesus Christ, by His death and resurrection, restored and re-established righteousness and holiness to man who believes.

A believer is a new creature in Christ; in him *old things (life of sin and wickedness) have come to an end.* Sin and death no longer rules and reigns over men who have given their lives to God. By Christ's work on the cross, believers have *become the righteousness of God in Christ, and partakers of God's holiness* (Heb. 12:10). A believer now has a new life.

We believers again have the personal responsibility and duty to maintain the holiness we have received from Christ (in other to succeed where the first Adam failed). That's why God continually urges us to put on the new man, which was re-created at new birth in holiness and righteousness. To do this, we must first put off the old man with his offending sinful nature (Eph. 4:22-24).

4. *Your body is the temple of Holy Spirit.* This is what the Bible says, and this means that the Spirit of God resides permanently in you (1 Cor. 6:19-20).
Your body being the temple of the Holy Spirit means that your body is the home of God's Spirit. What is the import of the above? As a believer, God dwells in you. Therefore, you are the house of God (Heb. 3:6).

Can the house where God dwells be anything but holy? Besides, Roman 1:4 calls the Holy Spirit the Spirit of Holiness. Shall the Spirit of Holiness dwell in unholy, unclean house? God forbids it. This is why holiness is a believer's responsibility – to maintain holiness and righteousness. The two cannot walk together except they are in agreement, the Scripture says (Amos 3:3).

Furthermore, an unbeliever is a property of the devil while a believer is a property of God, by reason of indwelling Holy Spirit. *You were bought at a price* of the precious blood of Jesus Christ. You have, therefore, the bounding duty to maintain that property in cleanness (holiness) for continual dwelling of God. And God warns, He will destroy that house if any man defiles it. 1 Cor. 3:16-17

Moreover, notice that the Bible says in 1 Cor. 6:11 that you w*ere washed, you were sanctif*ied… This means that you have been made holy as a believer through the new birth. This underscores the necessity, and responsibility for a believer to keep and maintain holiness.

God has cleaned you up for His holy habitation. Why become unclean (unholy) again?

5. *God calls believers saints.* Saints are not sinners. Saints are holy people who are pleasing to God, in whom God delights.

Believers are not and cannot be sinners because God calls them holy. A believer is not a sinner; he's a saint of God (Rom. 1:7; 1 Cor. 1:2).

As believers, we have a calling. As God called Abraham and he obeyed and followed, so also we have been called. Ours, primarily, is a call to holiness and righteousness; not to unholy and immoral living (1 Thess. 4:7).

We have personal responsibility as believers to maintain holiness. It's a great grace, and a great privilege that God, by His awesome power, has made us partakers of His holy nature. To keep that holiness, is a must for every believer.

Heb. 12:10, 14

10 For they indeed for a few days chastened us as seemed best to them, but He for our profit, that we may be partakers of His holiness. ...

14 Pursue peace with all people, and holiness, without which no one will see the Lord:

Pursue holiness, and don't become defiled, the Bible commands. In the Words of the Scripture, a believer must pursue holiness in all things.

6. *Holiness is the highway to glory and heaven.* God has shown again and again, that the pathway to heaven is holiness. It's also the pathway to glory and power in the ministry.

Without holiness, no man can make it to heaven. To make heaven is every believer's individual goal, pursuit and responsibility. God has shown the way, and that way is Christ – the key being holiness. Pursue peace and holiness. To pursue means to follow urgently with intent to capture; to aim for or go after.

I have a personal interpretation to Heb. 12:14. To follow or pursue peace with all men, means don't offend any man and don't allow any man offend you. It does not seem to be feasible or *do-able*.

Someone might say, you may be able to avoid offending people but you may not be able to stop people from offending you.

I say this to you. Your response to any offense or offending person is what determines whether an issue is an offense to you or not.

If you will learn to forgive every offender, and not keep an offense (or feel offended) you will have succeeded in this matter. We must continually forgive one another and not retain offense. (Eph. 4:32). It seems difficult but we have the help of the Spirit of Grace, the Holy Spirit.

That's why Paul could say, I have a conscience free of offense toward all men.

This being so, I myself always strive to have a conscience without offense toward God and men. (Acts 24:16).

No holiness, no heaven! 1 Tim 2:15

No one can be saved ultimately without holiness. To gain ultimate salvation (heaven), the key is holiness – not the works of the flesh. Gal 5:19-21

No one who practices sin, who works the works of the flesh, can make heaven. It's clear from the Scriptures above.

The talk of, once saved, saved forever, is a delusion of Satan; a doctrine of demons.

No one gets to heaven – God's abode - without holiness. God cannot compromise His holiness or lower His standard for anyone. He is not a respecter of any person. His law is His law – unchangeable and everlasting. And that's why He is a consuming fire despite being a God of mercy.

There is time for mercy, and there is time for judgment. When the time for mercy elapses, judgment follows.

As believers, the grace of this life we have is an opportunity for repentance, and for mercy. This is the dispensation of grace. A believer must make maximum use of this grace, so abundantly provided. Make determined effort to live holy and be pleasing to God.

How can Man keep and Maintain Holiness

Elijah had so much power with God in his ministry that his words carried great spiritual importance and weightiness. How did he wield so much power?

1 Kings 17:1

> **And Elijah the Tishbite, of the inhabitants of Gilead, said to Ahab, "As the Lord God of Israel lives, before whom I stand, there shall not be dew nor rain these years, except at my word."**

In the above declaration, Elijah ceased the rain over Israel for three and half years, even without praying or asking God. He committed God, Bible scholars say, and God honored his word.

What was Elijah's secret? *"As the Lord God of Israel lives, before whom I stand…."*

Elijah had a standing with God – I mean, he had power with God. And it was so because he was a holy and upright man according to Ps. 15. He was a man of integrity – a just and righteous man.

Psalm 15 presents us the secrets of power with God.

It's a great teaching on what a committed life of holiness means. That is the source of power, and the link to spiritual power. The presence of God is the place of power. Do you want power? Long and desire continually, the presence of God.

What should a man do to achieve holiness and maintain holiness?

- Walk uprightly (good morals and integrity)
- Work righteousness (have no fellowship with the works of the flesh (Gal. 5:19-21);
- Speak the truth always;
- Don't backbite; don't gossip;
- Think no evil and do no evil to a neighbor;
- Do no harm to a friend;
- Have no partnership with a vile person
- Honor those who fear God;
- Keep an oath or promise even when it hurts;
- Don't give or take bribe;
- Keep clean hands, and a pure heart;
- No perverse language;
- Walk in obedience (1 Pet. 1:14);
- Fear God – you perfect holiness through fear of God (1 Pet. 1:17; 2 Cor. 7:1; Eccl. 12:13);
- Offer your members as instruments of righteousness; not lending your mouth, your eyes or ears for evil use (Rom. 6:19).

Holiness is a major or key responsibility of believers. It's an on-going work – a continual daily spiritual exercise for a believer (1 Tim. 4:8).

Every believer must accept the spiritual responsibility of holiness – to live holy and keep holy. The house of the Lord must be holy continually. And you are that house.

Elijah was a man of like passion, but he had power with God. He spoke and Heaven upheld his word. All, because he was an upright, just and holy man. Will God hear your voice and uphold your word? The choice is yours.

What are the Blessings of Holiness?

- You will live perpetually in the presence of God;
- You become a vessel of honor for God's use;
- Your body becomes the perpetual abode of the Spirit of God;
- God will demonstrate his mightiness in you and through you;
- You become untouchable like the three Hebrew boys;
- Great miracles and signs will be wrought through you like Stephen and Paul;
- You word will carry power and commit God like Elijah (God will honor your word);
- All-round protection, and all-round blessing;
- God's glory will be all around you.

Walk in the Sprit

If we live in the Spirit, we must also walk in the Spirit (Gal. 5:25). That was Paul's exhortation to believers. To live and walk in the Spirit is to live Spirit-filled life. That is the calling of a believer.

What is Spirit-filled life? It's Spirit-led and controlled life; not one ruled and dominated by the flesh. As believers, we have the personal responsibility to mortify the flesh. We must not become debtors to the flesh to please the flesh on all fronts. Rom. 8:12-13

It's a Spirit-filled life, when by the mighty power that dwells in you, you are able to discipline the body and bring it into subjection (1 Cor. 9:27). The old man in you must die.

We must learn to put to death what the Bible calls our earthly enticing members: anger, malice, fornication, passion, evil desires, filthy language, covetousness and blasphemy (Col 3:5-11)

You have heard it! Put to death those patronizing members that conspire with Satan against the salvation of your soul. For a believer, there's really no other choice. Put off that old man and put on the new man recreated by the Holy Spirit at new birth (Eph. 4:22-24).

A Spirit-filled life also is a life full of joy; a thankful heart, and a submissive spirit (not headstrong or proud or obstinate). A Spirit-filled life makes holy living much more possible. Try it out.

APPENDIX 2

Spiritual Growth

Spiritual growth or growing up spiritually is another key responsibility of a believer. Physical and spiritual growths are similar, and have the same requirement.

A man who is not fed with food over time will die. Similarly, new born baby denied milk, cannot live. Food gives strength to the body and provides the needed ingredients for physical growth.

Just as an infant needs to grow, and requires physical food to grow, so every born again person (as a baby Christian) needs growth, and the spiritual food to grow.

In terms of provision, God has made adequate provisions for spiritual growth of every believer. But the responsibility to obtain and achieve spiritual growth rests with believers personally, and not with God.

How do we know that spiritual growth is a believer's responsibility?

1. *Spiritual Growth is God's command and Demand.*
    The Scriptures prove that God expressly made it so.
    1 Peter 2:2
    2 as newborn babes, desire the pure milk of the word, that you may grow thereby,

    NKJV used the word *desire*. But other versions elaborate further by saying *crave or thirst for.* This seems an instruction to a believer to long earnestly for the milk of the Word to grow.

    NKJV by emphatically saying, *desire the pure milk of the Word,* shows clearly that the ingredient (*spiritual food*) to execute the needed growth is the Word of God. The spiritual milk is the Word. The Word is the means and the instrument for growth.

    Believers should strive to grow in the grace and knowledge of Christ (2 Peter 3:18).

    Spiritual growth can be equated to growing in the knowledge of our Lord and Savior Jesus Christ. The means to growing in knowledge is the Word. If you feed on the Word of God, you will grow in knowledge. But if you fail to feed on the Word, you will not go far with God (Hosea 4:6).

Besides, the Scriptures give us insight into the reason for the command to feed on the pure milk of the word (the spiritual milk) to grow.

Other versions say in part, desire the spiritual milk that through it you may be nurtured, and grow up into fullness of salvation.

Therefore, baby Christians need to feed on the Word of God continually for the completion of their salvation (to come to the fullness of their salvation).

Paul exhorts Timothy to study in 2 Tim. 2:15.

Study! I see in that Scripture a command, and an instruction to somebody to fulfill a responsibility, an obligation or a duty. Why should we study? So that, by feeding on the Word of God (the spiritual milk), we may grow into mature Christians (no longer new born babes), but confident workers able to correctly handle the word of truth.

The additional understanding from the above is that, as mature Christians, we are better equipped and empowered (approved to God); made into vessels of honor for His holy use.

A baby Christian is not ready or equipped to be used of God or fit for God's use. He needs to mature and grow up to the standard of God's quality fitness. Or else he can't be used for the Master's work.

The foregoing shows that it's the believer's responsibility to grow spiritually.

2. *Consequences of not growing up spiritually* – there are dire consequences.

- Your salvation will be incomplete; and will not be in fullness (1 Pet. 2:2 AMP). You received salvation by hearing the Word (Rom. 10:17; 2 Tim. 3:1). The same token (the Word) is required to perfect your salvation. So grow in that Word.

- You run the risk of falling from your own steadfastness, which is Christ. 2 Peter 3:17

17 You therefore, beloved, since you know this beforehand, beware lest you also fall from your own steadfastness, being led away with the error of the wicked;

- One will be led away in error of the wicked. You will remember the Jonestown mass suicide and the Biblical example of Demas (2 Tim. 4:10). These people were led away into error. Mark 12:24 says,
24 Jesus answered and said to them, "Are you not therefore mistaken, because you do not know the Scriptures nor the power of God?

- Quarrelling about words or controversy over the Scriptures. Those who are not mature spiritually have the tendency to strive about words (2 Tim. 2:14)

- Carnality – one who refuses to feed on the Word of God, remains a perpetual baby Christian; flesh-ruled and flesh-led; strive-prone and unable to manifest the fruit of the spirit (Gal. 5:22-23). See also 1 Cor. 3:1-4 and Rom. 8:5-8.

Those who are in the flesh are carnal Christians, who have failed to grow by the reason of lack of exercises on the Word. Such cannot be pleasing to God.

What to Do to Grow Spiritually

Just as God has ordained in nature that infants should be nurtured and nourished to grow into mature adults physically, so He has too in the church (the body of Christ), that believers grow.

What provisions are there that God has made for believers' spiritual growth?

There are adequate provisions in the Word for the spiritual growth of believers in the church. God gave the ministry offices for this purpose (Eph. 4:11-15):

- Equipping of the saints (believers) for the work of the ministry
- For edifying (building up) of the body of Christ.
- For the unity of faith, and knowledge of Jesus Christ;
- For a believer to attain to a perfect man, to the measure of the stature of the fullness of Christ;
- For a believer to become grown up, no longer a baby Christian unable to correctly handle the Word;

- For believers to grow up in all things, dealing and speaking the truth in love.

There are certain instruments and institutions the church has put together (along with ministry gifts) to achieve the above objectives, namely:

- Sunday school
- House fellowship
- Weekly Bible study
- Believers' instructional class
- Devotionals and believer's own quiet time
- Conferences/Seminars
- Church vigils
- Inspired Christian literature/journals

God in His enduring wisdom has put all of the above for our spiritual growth. It's your responsibility as a believer to grow in knowledge and thereby complete your salvation.

The people of God are continually afflicted, and many are being destroyed for lack of knowledge according to Hos 4:6.

Don't be among those who are being destroyed due to ignorance or lack of knowledge. It is well within your ambit to do something about your spiritual growth. It is your personal responsibility.

Soul Winning

Yet another grave responsibility of a believer is soul winning.

God warned in the Old Testament times of the danger of allowing souls to die in sin. Prophets were the mouth-piece of God, and they had a responsibility, at the peril of their own lives, to warn backsliders and deliver them from hell.

Ezek. 33:7-11

> **7 "So you, son of man: I have made you a watchman for the house of Israel; therefore you shall hear a word from My mouth and warn them for Me.**
>
> **8 When I say to the wicked, 'O wicked man, you shall surely die!' and you do not speak to warn the wicked from his way, that wicked man shall die in his iniquity; but his blood I will require at your hand.**
>
> **9 Nevertheless if you warn the wicked to turn from his way, and he does not turn from his way, he shall die in his iniquity; but you have delivered your soul.**

10 "Therefore you, O son of man, say to the house of Israel: 'Thus you say, "If our transgressions and our sins lie upon us, and we pine away in them, how can we then live?"'**

11 Say to them: 'As I live,' says the Lord God, 'I have no pleasure in the death of the wicked, but that the wicked turn from his way and live. Turn, turn from your evil ways! For why should you die, O house of Israel?'**

The city's watchman has the grave responsibility to save lives by sounding the trumpet at the approach of danger or war (Ezek. 33:1-6). It's that same responsibility God vested on the prophets in order to save the lives of sinners. God has no desire or delight in a sinner going to hell. God's eternal will is that a sinner repents and makes heaven. That was the reason He invested the life of Jesus Christ to save the world.

The prophet of Old was not just a watchman to the nations, but also a guide to the people, to point them to righteousness, and to God (Isa 49:6).

In New Testament times, concerning the same matter, a believer stands in the place of the prophet of Old regarding the duty of the watchman. A believer is the watchman to the nations (unbelievers). A believer has a resident anointing (1 John 2:20, 27) like the prophet of Old, which qualifies and equips him for the role of a watchman.

Why is Soul Winning a Believer's Responsibility?

1. *Believers are harbingers of the good news of salvation.* Jesus Christ is the Author of salvation (Matt. 1:21; 20:28; John 3:16-18; 10:10). By His death and resurrection, Jesus has provided, and perfected and established salvation for all mankind (provisionally).

This good news, this wonder of a work, must be published, proclaimed and spread to all men – to the unsaved; that they may have the opportunity to receive salvation. (Salvation is deliverance from Satan's captivity, sin and hell through faith in Christ Jesus). God had assigned this task of spreading the good news to believers. We are to publish it. It's our assignment.

Matt 28:18-20

18 And Jesus came and spoke to them, saying, "All authority has been given to Me in heaven and on earth.

19 Go therefore and make disciples of all the nations, baptizing them in the name of the Father and of the Son and of the Holy Spirit,

20 teaching them to observe all things that I have commanded you; and lo, I am with you always, even to the end of the age." Amen.

And then the Bible warns further in Matt. 24:14 that when believers preach the gospel, it will be as a sign to all as a warning of the impending end.

2. *Believer as a Co-worker with God.* The witness of the Scripture confirms that God has graciously appointed believers as co-workers with Himself.

2 Cor. 6:1

We then, as workers together with Him also plead with you not to receive the grace of God in vain.

In what way has a believer become a partner and a fellow worker with God? For the saving of the souls of sinners (unbelievers). Believers are in partnership with God for the salvation of the world – as watchmen and carriers of the good news of salvation.

It's for this reason that believers are named disciples of Christ. Disciples are followers of Christ, who work with and work for Him to fulfill the will of God.

3. *The leave and authority to do greater works.* Jesus Christ before His departure from the earth, granted believers the permission and authority to perform greater works.

John 14:12

12 "Most assuredly, I say to you, he who believes in Me, the works that I do he will do also; and

greater works than these he will do, because I go to My Father.

Yes, believers will do greater works as Christ promised. But what could these greater works possibly be? Bible scholars say, these greater works include saving souls and delivering souls from hell, leading believers into the spiritual experience of the Holy Ghost baptism.

The greater works is not for the believer himself or the benefit of a believer. It's to continue Christ's work of bringing God's love into men's heart, changing men from being enemies of God into friendship with God (Jas. 4:4); granting them the power to become sons of God (John 1:12). It's also to turn the world upside down for God, that He may rule and reign in the hearts of men, and in the kingdoms of the world.

These are not the works for Christ to do; the crucial, the extraordinary, and the impossible He had done by dying on the cross for sinners. The greater works are rather, works believers must do for Christ, to arrest or stem the tide of millions of souls flowing to hell daily. For this reason, soul winning is believer's inescapable responsibility.

4. *Certain fearful expectation of loss and divine judgment.* There is a grave risk and danger to a believer who fails or refuses to evangelize or win souls. Concerning

soul winning, there's a reward for faithfulness just as there is a loss for failure. Ezek. 33:7-9

The Scripture says a believer who fails or refuses to win soul is guilty of blood. Why would a believer suffer blood-guiltiness or a loss?

To answer the above question we need to probe to understand the purpose of a believer's salvation. Why is a believer saved? Is it just to go to heaven?

First, we need to understand the fate of an unbeliever. An unbeliever is accursed and doomed. The implications of this are that (1) he has a perverted destiny, that is, he can never fulfill God's original vision (agenda) for his life; (2) spiritually speaking, he's completely barren and unfruitful; (3) His works in life no matter how great, have no eternal reckoning and value; (4) His name is recorded in the enemy's journals of death (not in the Lamb's book of life); (5) He's programmed for destruction (Rom. 9:22; Ps. 92:7); (6) He will never see God but will rather perish in the lake of fire (Rev. 21:8); (7) He's completely hopeless in this life; a stranger to God, and an alien to ways of or things of God (Eph. 2:12); (8) above all, he is spiritually dead. Curses will trail him, pursue him and overtake him. The Bible says, he shall be cursed all round (Deut. 28:15-21).

But when a sinner gives his life to Christ and becomes born again, then the opposite of all we have said above will count for him. He will be made spiritually fruitful and blessed all around (Deut. 28:1-14). In fact, blessings will follow him, pursue him and overtake him.

But the key point is this, a believer is not saved just to be blessed and go to heaven. A believer is a seed of corn God has planted through Christ.

What does a planted seed of corn brings, in harvest? Several seeds; multiple grains; many ears or cobs of corn. It's a multiplication.

This is the physical law that governs the earth. It's just the natural law. A planted seed of corn will never give back just one seed. It either gives multiple grains as nature commands or it dies not producing anything at all.

Spiritually speaking, a believer is a planted seed of corn. He has a choice to reproduce self in multiples or dies.

The implication of this is that a believer who is not winning soul may lose heaven. Because he has defied the natural law or God's command to be fruitful (that is, to reproduce himself).

God chose you and empowered you to bear fruit. To do otherwise, amounts to rebellion. Doesn't it? Besides, bearing fruit (in other words winning soul) is part of obeying the New Commandment of love.

Therefore, a believer who fails to bear fruit is defying, frustrating and opposing divine order or command. This is gross disobedience; such a believer may end up in hell (Luke 13:6-9).

Even the statement of Jesus toward the end of His life on earth, in the gospel of John chapter fifteen, is very fearful.

John 15:1-2

I I am the true vine, and My Father is the vinedresser.

2 Every branch in Me that does not bear fruit He takes away; and every branch that bears fruit He prunes, that it may bear more fruit.

Hear this, *every branch that does not bear fruit, He takes away.* To be taken away means to be cut off. A branch cut off from a tree withers and dies. It's a great warning to believers.

Now, we cannot bear fruit until we abide in Christ. To abide in Christ is to receive salvation – to be born again.

Once you are born again you're abiding in Christ, and have received power to bear fruit. But if you fail, verse 6 warns that one will be cast out as a branch, and gathered into the fire, and be burnt.

A believer who is not bearing fruit (winning soul) runs the risk of losing heaven, and may go to hell.

A believer is saved purposely to save others. This makes soul winning a major responsibility of a believer.

5. *It's God's Command* – soul winning is God's command to believers. This command is contained in His Word (the Scriptures).

Prov. 11:30

30 The fruit of the righteous is a tree of life, and he who wins souls is wise.

God is the Author of wisdom (Jas. 13:13-17). Believers are re-created, born of the Spirit of wisdom, and therefore, has access to divine wisdom. Thus, believers need not act foolishly by not winning soul. Our Father is the Author of wisdom – we must walk in that wisdom He has given. For a believer, wisdom is the principal thing for living. And he that wins soul is wise. Prov. 24:11

11 Deliver those who are drawn toward death, and hold back those stumbling to the slaughter.

Who are *those drawn to death? Stumbling to fire, to slaughter?* Sinners, the unbelievers! And what is the command to believers, *hold them back, deliver them!*

The import of what God is saying in the Scriptures, and in Ezek. 33:8-9, is that *the ultimate salvation of a believer is tied inseparably to the salvation of other souls God has attached to the believer's life. A believer is the watchman to the nations (sinners).*

What are the other Scriptures commanding soul winning or evangelization?

Matt. 28:18-19

18 And Jesus came and spoke to them, saying, "All authority has been given to Me in heaven and on earth.

19 Go therefore and make disciples of all the nations, baptizing them in the name of the Father and of the Son and of the Holy Spirit,

Bible scholars call the above the Great Commission. It's a commission which a believer is *commissioned, appointed, chosen, ordained and anointed* to deliver to the world (the unsaved) at the risk or peril of his salvation or his life (Ezek. 33:7;8). Should we fail God in this all-important assignment? Never!

Believers have been chosen before the foundation of the world to bear abiding fruits, and to do greater works.

Jude 22-23

22 And on some have compassion, making a distinction;

23 but others save with fear, pulling them out of the fire, hating even the garment defiled by the flesh.

The divine command is quite clear – *have Christ-like compassion, save others, pull the dying multitude out of the fire of hell.* God commands it.

Soul winning is an act of mercy; an act in mercy, and a work of mercy.

God has shown you who believes, such a great mercy you don't deserve. Where is your mercy toward sinners? Where is your compassion for the perishing souls, when you refuse to share the good news with them?

God wants the whole world to be saved. And that's why He has chosen you. Time is running out – let's not fail God. In this all-important business which is soul winning, your modest effort and contribution count.

Soul winning is not only an act of mercy; it's doing the work of reconciliation as ambassadors of Christ. It's our calling as believers. As believers, we are reconciled with God through Christ, and it's our duty to bring others into that same spiritual experience and blessing. 2 Cor. 5:18-21

God is indeed, pleading through us for the saving of souls. He has given us the *Word of reconciliation* saying, 'get them reconciled; bring them out of darkness into the light'.

And for those who accept this invitation and command, there are diverse blessings: you won't labor in vain but will enjoy divine presence and support (1 Chron. 28:20).

Besides, your salvation will be established, and you will reign with the King of kings with crown of rejoicing (1 Thess. 2:19). The Lord will reward you greatly (Rev. 22:12).

APPENDIX 4

Giving

Many Christians do not see giving as a responsibility, a duty or an obligation they need to perform. They don't see it as anything that could affect their lives, or a possible answer to the greatest quest of life. This could be as a result of ignorance or lack of understanding of the Word of God, and the ways of God.

To say the least, giving is one of the major responsibilities of Christians. It's a work every believer must do; it's an obligation a true Christian must perform.

Why is giving a major responsibility of a believer?

To understand this matter very well, we must know that God is a God of precepts and principles (Isa. 28:10). God works by principles. He is not an arbitrary Spiritual Being; nor author of confusion. If you understand the Word of God, on the general note, you can predict God. For the Word of God is the will of God.

What do I mean by that? If you're obedient, there's little that can stop you from enjoying good things (God's blessings). Also, if you decide to live immoral life, you will be sure you will end up in hell. But, if you live holy, you're sure of heaven. It's as simple as that.

Besides, God who created man, made him for a purpose. It's not for adversity; it's for ultimate good and peace.

God did not create man to suffer and sorrow through life. He made man to be great and successful in life,

God has interest and pleasure in a man being great and successful. Adam was not created a suffering and sorrowing man – he was made great, powerful and successful. But sin in him made the difference.

God made known His resolve and commitment to make man successful, when He spoke to children of Israel in the wilderness. And He told them categorically that He is the God who gives them the power to prosper and succeed (Deut 8:18).

Yes, God gives power to get wealth. Why does God give His people power to prosper? It's so because He's committed to their well-being and prosperity.

God does not only give the power of wealth, the Bible says He teaches a believer to profit (Isa. 48:17). He shows a believer the pathways and the conditions to obtain success. Through Christ, He redeemed believers from every curse of the law; and gives us a gracious part in the blessings of Abraham. In Christ, believers' prosperity is assured as we see in the following Scriptures.

2 Cor. 8:9

> **9 For you know the grace of our Lord Jesus Christ, that though He was rich, yet for your sakes He became poor, that you through His poverty might become rich.**

Man's success and prosperity is God's deliberate plan and purpose – His design and delight. The above Scriptures demonstrate this divine intent.

Then, because God is interested in the success of man (the crown of His creation), He personally instituted plans, guidelines, paths and the conditions to that greatness and success.

What is the path-way to divine prosperity?

1. *Obedience* - obey God in all things, fully, totally and completely. This is number one requirement. Obedience brings about peace, long life and fruitfulness (Deut. 6:2-3; Isa. 1:19).

Job 36:11-12

> **11 If they obey and serve Him, they shall spend their days in prosperity, and their years in pleasures.**
>
> **12 But if they do not obey, they shall perish by the sword, and they shall die without knowledge.**

Yes, obey; obey and obey. It's about obedience. But to this you must add other important requirements.

2. *Giving* – giving is one of the ways God has established to bless His people. Giving attracts and generates prosperity, as sowing attracts and generates harvest.

   In God's Word, we have assurance of harvest for our sowing. It's the natural law. A farmer who sows cannot be in want of harvest.

   Harvest is a natural outcome of sowing. As harvest is a consequence of sowing, so prosperity is the consequence of giving. It's also a spiritual law, and that's how God has instituted it. Seedtime and harvest time shall never cease, as the earth remains

   God wants His people to increase and prosper, and He has laid down this principle, in place to bless His people. It may sound paradoxical, but the Bible says to increase you must scatter (Prov. 11:24-25).

   He that scatters is he that gives; scattering (giving) brings about increase (prosperity). And the reverse is true; not giving (being stingy, withholding) leads to poverty.

   A good example of the positive side of this principle is King Solomon. The King, in one day, in one fell swoop, offered to God one thousand offerings, and the result was predictably wonderful. 2 Chron. 1:6-12

Solomon gave – he gave his best: a thousand burnt offerings in one day. And God responded dramatically with uncommon pronouncement of uncommon blessings (v. 11-12). God gave King Solomon a blank check to demand whatever he pleased. In a way, we might say Solomon surprised God with his giving, and God surprised him with great blessings.

God, again and again, has shown clearly and openly to the church (Old and New) His plans of prosperity; that giving is His deliberate plan, and articulated method to bless His people. God wants His people to prosper, and He continually points to giving as the door that leads to the prosperity.

Zech. 1:17

17 "Again proclaim, saying, 'Thus says the Lord of hosts:" My cities shall again spread out through prosperity; The Lord will again comfort Zion, And will again choose Jerusalem.""

The prosperity of God's kingdom (My cities) is the prosperity of His people (believers). It's through the prosperity of believers that the kingdom of God (the church) will prosper. This will be realized thorough obedience to the command to give.

Luke 6:38

38 Give, and it will be given to you: good measure, pressed down, shaken together, and running over will be put into your bosom. For with the same measure that you use, it will be measured back to you."

When you give, how shall it be given to you in return? In good great measure (pressed down, and shaken together, and running over).

Giving is the key to overflowing prosperity. Giving is the route to prosperity beyond measure; it's the pathway to exceeding multiplication and abundant, unlimited blessing or wealth.

King Solomon's example has a lot to teach us on this subject. Out of his giving, and because of his giving, God gave him wealth in dimensions that no man had ever had before him and would ever have after him.

King Solomon did not do any other thing other than he gave, and gave extraordinarily. And God blessed him extraordinarily with overflowing riches and wealth, and unparalleled wisdom.

A man, who gives, is like a farmer who sows seeds. Can a farmer who plants a field, lack harvest, as the earth remains? (Gen 8:22). No!

Every sowing has a promise of harvest. Sowing as giving is the key to great harvest or overflowing prosperity.

A farmer who sows bountifully would in return receive bountiful, overflowing harvest (2 Cor. 9:6-8).

Generous giving is a key to overflowing prosperity. God who gives the increase to every sowing act (giving) is well able to channel all grace to your work, and give you all sufficiency, in all things for abundance and overflow of wealth.

God desires and determines that His people prosper. It's not only His desire; He has planned it out, and ordained it to happen. But your prospering is tied to your giving; it's in giving that you are blessed (Acts 20:35). God has made it so.

This is why giving is a believer's responsibility. It's what you must necessarily do for yourself. God gives the complementary act – the grant of grace to prosper.

God is waiting for your prosperity as a believer, because it's through it He will *spread His cities abroad* (Zech. 1:17).

Your prosperity as a believer brings God glory. Our poverty does not honor God, but prosperity does. God is the Author of prosperity and not poverty; Satan is the author of it (poverty).

The earth and the fullness thereof belong to God (Ps. 24:1; Hag. 2:8). Believers' prosperity is God's delight and design. Believers' prosperity honors God and brings Him glory. And the key to a believer's prosperity is giving (and sowing). This is the reason why giving is one of the major responsibilities of a believer.

Now when we talk about giving what are we to give? Materials and money as directed by the Scriptures, namely: offerings (Deut. 16:16-17); tithes (Mal. 3:8-12); first fruits (Prov. 3:9-10); giving to needy folks (Prov. 19:17; Rom. 12:13; Gal. 6:10; 1 Tim. 5:17-19); giving to church and programs – sowing (Zech. 1:17; 2 Cor. 9:6).

APPENDIX 5

Growing Your Faith

Growing your faith, making your faith deeper and stronger is one of your major personal responsibilities, as a believer.

What is faith?

- Faith is, believing that God exists, and that He is who He says He is; and He is a rewarder of those who seek after Him.
- Faith is, trusting absolutely on God that He unfailingly will do what He says He would do.
- Faith is holding into God's Word to be true even when the circumstances speak to the contrary.
- Faith is being absolutely convinced that it's impossible for God to lie, and that His Word will perform that which He sent it to do (Isa. 55:11);
- Faith is the reality of what we hope for, being in possession of proof of what we don't see;
- Faith is our handle on what we can't see.
- Faith is confidence in what we are hoping for, the assurance of the reality we currently do not see.
- Faith is what makes real the things we hope for.
- Faith is knowing that something is real even if we do not see it, and being sure of what we hope for.

- Faith is God's currency of spiritual transaction, and without it, no believer can do business with God (Heb. 11:6).
- Faith is the fulcrum upon which a believer's relationship with God thrives. It's one of the key determinants of our standing with God.
- Faith together with holiness is the spiritual ladder with which to climb up to the abode of God.
- Faith is what compels God's hand of power and miracle to your favor,

It's your personal responsibility as a believer to grow your faith. A responsibility is what you do by yourself and for yourself – not what God does for you.

God cannot and will not grow your faith for you. You have to do it yourself. It's your duty, your obligation and commitment as a believer.

Let's look at some of the Scriptural proofs that confirm that growing your faith is a personal responsibility.

God commands it.

The following Scriptures are not appeal or advice but rather express divine command.

Deut. 6:5

> **5 You shall love the Lord your God with all your heart, with all your soul, and with all your strength.**

You shall love the Lord. It sounds like an appeal, but it is God's command to us. You must love God because in it is your peace. Besides, you cannot love what you don't believe in and cherish. The command to love God is a command to trust or believe God.

Prov. 3:5-6

> **5 Trust in the Lord with all your heart, and lean not on your own understanding;**

> **6 In all your ways acknowledge Him, and He shall direct your paths.**

The persistent call or command to trust the Lord is an invitation to exercise your faith in God.

How does a muscle builder increase or add on muscle? By persistent, continual exercise or work out. Likewise, we grow our faith by continually trusting and believing God and His Word, and acting on His Word.

By continual call to trust God, God is deliberately bringing us into the arena of faith growth by that spiritual exercise.

We see the same call to faith-growth targeted exercises in Mark 11:22. It enjoins us to have faith in God.

To have faith in God or have God's kind of faith is an invitation to grow your faith. You can't give what you don't have. To have God's kind of faith, you need to develop it or grow it. Then you can exercise it.

We also see this same call to grow faith in Jude 20, where it says, you edify your faith by praying in the Holy Spirit.

I see this as a direct, express command to grow your faith. The passage is asking believers to build themselves up and be strong through faith. Faith, it can be said, is a measure of believer's strength in Christ. A man of great faith, like Stephen, is a man who is powerful in the Lord – a man who has power with God.

It was said of Stephen, that he was full of faith and the Holy Spirit, and that God did mighty signs and wonders through him (Acts 6:5, 8).

Without Faith no one can Please God

The Bible has stated it categorically. Without faith, you cannot please God (Heb. 11:6). It's impossible to please God if you're walking in unbelief, and not in faith.

Without faith, a believer cannot be a co-worker with God nor do the works that Christ did (1 Cor. 3:9; John 14:12). We need God's kind of faith to walk the walk.

Though, a believer is saved through faith in Christ (Eph. 2:8; Rom. 10:9, 10), yet if you don't grow your faith, you won't go far with God. Your faith must grow beyond the saving faith, so to speak.

As a believer, you must not stop at the first rung of the ladder. Climb up higher, take more steps up – develop the mustard seed-kind of faith. That's the faith that pleases God, and that provokes the miraculous in signs and wonders. That's where a believer belongs. But without faith you can't please God nor provoke miracles. You develop this kind of faith by firmly holding onto God's Word without wavering – if God has said it, it must be true, it can't fail. Go out with that confidence, act on the Word and expect it to work.

A Natural Necessity.

A growth in faith is a natural necessity for every believer. It's natural that a new born baby grows. But if the baby rejects food and would not eat, naturally, it would die. And so it is for a new born babe in Christ (a believer). As it is natural for a new born baby to grow, so it is for a believer.

A believer must grow in faith in order to be alive in Christ and for Christ. As the Bible says, it's in Christ that we live and move and have our being (Acts 17:28). Only faith makes that possible. Without faith, a believer will perish.

It's not God's duty to grow your faith as a believer; it's your personal responsibility.

What did faith do to the three Hebrew boys? It preserved their lives and made them a wonder to their generation (Daniel chapter three).

What did faith do for Abraham? It made him a father of the nations; a blessing to the whole world; it made him a friend of God, and kept him in God's everlasting memory and reckoning (Gen. 12:1-3; 17:1-12).

What did faith did for Daniel? It shut the mouths of the lions for his deliverance and safety; gave him divine approval, protection and promotion for a colorful career that spanned over four dynasties of Babylon.

What did lack of faith do for Esau? He lost his inheritance, and as well, a prime position in the revered lineage and genealogy that gave the world Jesus Christ.

What are the Benefits of Growing your Faith?

1. Abraham believed God and it was accounted unto him for righteousness, so will a believer with Abraham-kind of faith, receive and be established in righteousness (Gen. 15:6).
2. It will make you well pleasing to God, and it will keep you in God's everlasting friendship and reckoning (Heb. 11:6).
3. It will preserve your life and perfect your salvation (1 Pet. 2:2 AMP).
4. You will become a vessel of honor with which God will wrought mighty signs and wonders (Acts 6:8).
5. It will terminate fear from your life like the three Hebrew boys; and apostle Paul who was ever ready to allow his life to be poured out like a libation for the sake of the gospel (2 Tim. 4:6).
6. It will bring about a joyful life through answered prayers

How to Grow your Faith

Every believer must accept the spiritual responsibility to grow his faith. Like a young plant in a nursery, give it necessary ingredients, and you see it growing and thriving. A believer's faith must grow and thrive. How?

1. *By feeding on the Word of God daily.* Daily meditation on the Word of God is akin to a gold-smith fanning the ambers of the flame. What happens? As he fans the flame, it grows and glows. Rom. 10:17 says faith comes by hearing the Word of God. By that same Word, in continual reading and meditation, faith grows and deepens. The Word grows faith. Feeding and meditating on the Word of God is a believer's personal responsibility, and it brings about both spiritual growth and faith growth. God commands it (Josh 1:8; Ps 1:1-3)

   Yes, it's God's command that a believer meditate on the Word at least twice daily, and as well, do the Word continually (Jas. 1:22-23). In these are the believer's blessings.

2. *By Praying in the Holy Ghost.* Praying in tongues (that is, praying in the Holy Ghost) is a spiritual exercise that does great good in strengthening believer's faith (Jude 20).

   Yes, praying in the Holy Spirit edifies your faith. To edify means to build up; to charge up. In the natural, when you charge up an automobile battery, you increase it in power. That's precisely what praying in the Holy Spirit does to your faith. It builds you up – it increases you in spiritual strength and power.

Believers should pray often in the Holy Spirit. When you pray in tongues, you are communicating mysteries (secrets) that only God understands. Besides the fact that it opens you up to divine revelations, it's a spirit-to-spirit communication that draws you closer into the arena of the perfect will of God ((Rom. 8:26-27).

God through the Holy Spirit gives us the knowledge of His holy will; wisdom and discernment is given to us to walk according to His good pleasure with understanding of His plans and purposes for our lives (Eph. 1:9; Phil 1:9-11).

Believers do have access to the knowledge of the mystery of God's will. Praying in tongues brings you to the center of the leadership of the Holy Spirit into that will.

When we pray in the Holy Spirit, the Spirit helps us to pray, He guides us into the perfect will of God. And if it is the Holy Spirit who is leading you, He cannot lead you away from God's holy will but direct into it

Believers should pray more in the Holy Spirit. It's a great and beautiful way to pray.

I share with you the testimony of a mother of three which I read some time ago. At about noon, while the children were away to school, this young mother was in the kitchen doing the dishes. Suddenly she felt an intense urge to pray. Unable to resist it, she turned aside and knelt beside the dining table. Not knowing what exactly to pray, she yielded to the Holy Spirit and began to intercede in tongues. After a considerable length of time, she had a relief in her spirit and she went back to the kitchen.

Now, well after an hour or so, the children came back from school a bit agitated. And they began to tell their mother how a driver lost control of a vehicle and came straight at Junior on the side curb, who was miraculously lifted up from the spot unscathed. But for that inexplicable call to prayer, Junior, her youngest son would have been killed.

It takes cooperation with the Spirit of God to avert such dangers. But would we be sensitive enough to heed His calling to pray when He does call?

3. *Fellowship in a Bible-believing (Full Gospel) Church.* The church is the ground and pillar of truth (1 Tim. 3:15). Not that the church is the source of truth, Jesus Christ is; He is the Truth. But the church being the body of believers is the Body of Christ, to which Christ is the Head. Physically, the head is the seat of the government of the body – it directs all the functions of the body. This is what, makes the

church the ground and the pillar of truth because Christ who is her Head is the Truth (John 14:6).

The church is the place where the truth (God's whole counsel as revealed in His Word) abides and is taught correctly, and practiced. This describes a full-gospel church. And the Bible warns, *forsake not such gathering* (Heb. 10:25).

Fellowshipping in a full-gospel church will expose you to the truth – the correct Word of God. Not to dogmas, man-made philosophies or extra-biblical (non-scriptural) doctrines or traditions of men.

A full gospel church is a church that draws all her doctrines from the Bible alone – uncontaminated with traditions and patriarchal directives or orders. Paul assured the Corinthians, that his preaching was not with persuasive words of human wisdom, but with power and wisdom that only the Holy Spirit gives (1 Cor. 2:4-5).

Your faith as a believer should not be in the wisdom of men but in the power of God.

When you receive constantly right teaching, correct Word of God, your faith will escalate – it will grow and deepen.

Any seed you plant in a bad soil, you have killed *ab initio*. As a believer, be sure you are in the right environment – in the correct church that teaches and practices the word; the ground and pillar of truth, that is, a true harbinger of truth. A believer in a wrong environment (a church that does not teach the whole truth) cannot grow in faith. Faith comes and grows by the correct Word of God. How do you know the right environment? Check out all the teachings and doctrines of the church, and compare by what the Bible says. Do they align? Do they agree? Acts 17:10-11

10 Then the brethren immediately sent Paul and Silas away by night to Berea. When they arrived, they went into the synagogue of the Jews. 11 These were more fair-minded than those in Thessalonica, in that they received the word with all readiness, and searched the Scriptures daily to find out whether these things were so.

They searched the Scriptures daily to find out whether these things were so. A believer has the duty to search or else be 'rail-roaded' into oblivion.

4. *Read Sound Christian Literature or Titles.* Read with discernment any great popular Christian authors on diverse subjects. The Holy Spirit has been working through so many anointed Christian authors, who have produced great books to the glory of God. Read as many as you can. This personally has helped me a great deal in growing my faith. I am an avid reader, and I read with discerning and critical (questioning) mind.

My journey into divine health started with the testimony I read about a Pastor. My faith also received a big boost through my readings of other great authors.

5. *Listen to Testimonies* – testimonies are a great tonic to our faith journey. They remind us continually of the great power of the God of awesome wonders; that God is still in the business of doing great miracles and wonders; that our miracles are the next on the line. Your expectations shall not be cut off (Ps. 9:18; Prov. 23:18).

6. *Act on the Word*. Whatever the Word of God says, believe it and act on the word – act on it as if it is true. We walk by faith not by sight. You activate your faith by acting on the Word, and as you do, you will get results.

Apostle Paul prayed for the Thessalonians thus: "*We are bound to thank God always for you, brethren, as it is fitting, because your faith grows exceedingly, and the love of every one of you all abounds toward each other,*" (2 Thess. 1:3).

I pray for you, too. May your faith grow exceedingly, and may you be rooted and grounded in Christ's love.

APPENDIX 6

Walk in Love

Therefore be imitators of God as dear children. 2 And walk in love, as Christ also has loved us and given Himself for us, an offering and a sacrifice to God for a sweet-smelling aroma.

Eph. 5:1-2

Walking in love is one of the major responsibilities of a believer. It's a duty we must do; an obligation we must observe; a task we must perform; work we must work.

It's not a matter of choice; it's a commitment we are committed with. In it lays our peace; upon it shall our Christian life thrive and succeed. Walking in love is a principal thing; a divine demand.

In the Old Testament time, Israel in the wilderness received the Law of Moses, which includes the Ten Commandment (Exod. 10:1-17).

These were ordinances, statutes and decrees they were commanded to observe, obey and follow at all times, before and after their settlement in the Promised Land. The laws affected every area of their lives, and they were binding to them.

The Ten Commandment and the accompanying moral laws and ceremonial laws were given specifically to the Jews – only to the Jews. They were not given to the Gentiles, and the Gentiles were not bound by them.

However, Christians (whether Jews or Gentiles) are not under the law. The law was given only to the Jews, as their tutor and guard, pending the time when the promised deliverer (Jesus Christ) would appear (Gal 3:23-25).

With the coming of faith (meaning Jesus Christ) New Testament believers are justified, not by keeping the law, but by faith in Christ. Believers are no longer under the tutor (the Law).

Moses had said to the Jews concerning the Law, he who keeps the law shall live. The people were justified by keeping the law – they obtain justice in the law or by keeping and living the law.

But believers are not under the law – they are freed from the Law, and they are not bound to observe it nor keep it. Believers are under grace (Rom. 6:14).

Believers are dead to the Law – divorced from the Law and married to Christ Jesus. Christ stands both for the fulfillment of the Law and the end of the Law. The law leads up to Christ, and in Him its purposes were fulfilled. Thus, those who have put their faith in Christ are freed from the Law (Rom. 7:4-6; 10:4).

The purpose of the Law in its entirety was fulfilled in Christ, and Christ alone. As New Testament believers, we are no longer required to obey the Law to live or be justified. Christ is our justification – He's the means to a believer's justification or righteousness. We are justified by faith in Christ. That's why a believer is not under the Law.

A New Commandment

Believers are under grace or under the dispensation of grace. The Law was given through Moses, but grace and truth came through Jesus Christ (John 1:17).

Dispensation of grace signifies that believers are freely justified by grace through faith in Christ apart from the law (Rom. 5:1). Believers don't have to keep the law to live. Believers live, and are saved by grace through faith in Christ (Eph. 2:8).

Christ is the end of the law for us who believe. But before Christ departed from the earth, He gave a New Commandment to the church.

John 13:34-35

> **34 A new commandment I give to you, that you love one another; as I have loved you, that you also love one another.**
>
> **35 By this all will know that you are My disciples, if you have love for one another."**

Believers have received a new commandment. Believers are not under the Law of Moses (the Ten Commandment inclusive), we are under a new command – the Commandment of love.

I give to you a New Commandment that you love one another…

That's why Paul exhorted the church, *be imitators of God; walk in love.*

It is, therefore, the personal responsibility of every believer to walk in love. All the requirement of the Law is fulfilled just in one word, love (Gal 5:14; Rom 13:8-10).

Divine Enablement

Every believer has divine enablement to perform this duty – walking in love. First of all, the Bible says God is love (1 John 4:8). In other words, God has the divine nature of love. And every man who is born again is born of God. That means a believer is born of love because God is love. So believers have the God's love nature in them. God is love and His love nature dwells in a believer. This I consider a primary divine motivation for believers to walk in love.

Secondly, the Bible says that God has shed His love upon our hearts. This happens at new birth. The divine love of God, agape love, is in the heart of every believer at the time he is born again, because as we said earlier, he is born of love (of God, who is love). Rom 5:5

Because God's love has been poured into our hearts, you would imagine that, to walk in love ought to be as natural to a believer as breathing. However, we don't need any special preparation or impartation. All that a believer needs, is to allow the Spirit to dominate him, and not allow the flesh to rule over him. In such a setting, the God's love nature will begin to manifest. Wake up to it; begin this walk of love now as you open yourself up to the Holy Spirit.

Character of Love

Here, we are discussing God kind of love, agape love; not the world kind of love expressed as erotic love or any other kind.

For one to adequately understand the command to walk in love, we need to know the character of agape love.

Paul's first epistle to the Corinthians, enumerates elaborately and diligently, the noble character of Christian love, agape love (1 Cor. 13:4-8).

The passages describe in detail what it means to walk in love. He who walks in love cannot be rude nor provoked; he would not think nor speak evil against a brother or a sister; he will always believe the best (not evil) for brethren; he is ever ruled by patience and a heart of kindness. Apostle Paul calls it the excellent way (1 Cor. 12:31).

To walk in love is not just the excellent way, but a major responsibility of a believer. Besides being God's commandment to a believer, another reason why we should walk in love is because love covers multitudes of sins. So Apostle Peter exhorts the brethren, to have fervent love for one another, and serve one another in love (1 Peter 4:7-11).

God has loved us so much – even beyond measure, though, undeserving as we are. Brethren ought to love one another. This is what it means to walk in love.

To every believer, the key to victorious Christian life is in living up to our personal responsibilities in the Lord. If we do these things willingly, there are certain rewards to receive (1 Cor. 9:17).

I have never seen a believer who lives up to the above billings, who is forgotten or abandoned by the Lord.

David the Psalmist said in all his life, he had not seen the righteous forsaken or his children begging for bread (Ps. 34:8-10).

We can summarize the responsibility to walk in love as follows:

What is love?"
- Love is patient, love is kind

What love is not?
- Puffed up
- Self-seeking
- Easily provoked

What love does?
- Hopes all
- Believes all
- Bears all

- Endures all

What love does not?
- Vaunt itself
- Envy
- Behave itself rudely
- Rejoices in iniquity
- Thinks evil
- Fails

Love is an action in reality. It's much more of an action than a feeling.

Love covers the multitudes of sins. Therefore, walk in love and live.

APPENDIX 7

Payer

Prayer is yet another major responsibility of a believer. It's a spiritual exercise that connects a believer to God, and provides a divine platform for spiritual intercourse (of fellowship and communication). We communicate and fellowship with God when we pray (1 John 1:3).

Prayer is divine because God is Spirit, who longs for our worship, which the medium of prayer facilitates. Prayer is a serious responsibility of a believer because God longs and looks forward to it (John 4:23).

John 4:23-24

> **23 But the hour is coming, and now is, when the true worshipers will worship the Father in spirit and truth; for the Father is seeking such to worship Him.**
>
> **24 God is Spirit, and those who worship Him must worship in spirit and truth."**

Men Ought to Pray

God decided from the very beginning to have fellowship with man. Early in creation, He provided that platform, opportunity and privilege. The Bible says God visited Adam and Eve in the *cool of the day* at the Garden of Eden. That's why a believer's prayer life is a hallmark of intimacy and fellowship with God.

Men ought to pray! Back in Egypt in the days of their servitude and bondage, the continual cry of Israel through prayer was a constant reminder to God of His promise of deliverance to Abraham His friend. And that deliverance came at the end of 430 years bondage.

Again, back at the wilderness, after the Red Sea miracle, it was the prayer of Moses that saved the young nation of Israel from divine judgment (Exod. 32).

Prayer avails much. And Jesus says believers ought to pray (Luke 18:1-2).

The unrelenting prayer of the un-named woman turned the situation around for her. Men ought to pray and not lag in diligence, but be fervent in the spiritual exercise of prayer.

The Command to Pray

God desires to do great things on the earth for His glory and for the blessings of our lives. But these wonders will not happen unless men would pray.

2 Chron. 7:14

14 if My people who are called by My name will humble themselves, and pray and seek My face, and turn from their wicked ways, then I will hear from heaven, and will forgive their sin and heal their land.

God is ever ready to heal our land, and cause our land to yield her increase and bring forth divine wonders. Bur men must learn to pray and worship His Majesty (Ps 67:5-7).

Because righteous prayer is God's delight, Jesus Christ, late in His ministry, set the agenda and gave the following instructions.

John 16:23-24

23 "And in that day you will ask Me nothing. Most assuredly, I say to you, whatever you ask the Father in My name He will give you.

24 Until now you have asked nothing in My name. Ask, and you will receive, that your joy may be full.

These texts gave the right agenda. This is how a believer should pray – you ask the Father in the name of Jesus Christ. Not in the name of an angel or any man or woman (dead or living). All prayer is to God the Father in Jesus name.

Jesus also added another refreshing dimension in the following Scriptures.

John 14:13-14

> **13 And whatever you ask in My name, that I will do, that the Father may be glorified in the Son.**
>
> **14 If you ask anything in My name, I will do it.**

Bible scholars say that the word "ask" in John 14:13-14 means *demand* in Greek text. Therefore, verse 14 can be read as, "… whatever you DEMAND in my name that I will do …"

A good example of this is found in the story of a lame man at the Beautiful Gate (Acts 3:1-8). Look closely and you will see that apostle Peter did not pray. Rather he demanded in the name of Jesus that the lame man walk. And he that was lame, stood up, walked, leaped and danced giving glory to God.

There are so many directives about prayer in the Bible. Let's look at more.

1 Tim. 2:1

> **Therefore I exhort first of all that supplications, prayers, intercessions, and giving of thanks be made for all men,**

Believers are commanded to pray for all men and for those in authority (kings, presidents or heads of government), for peace of life and God's blessings.

A believer praying is God's delight; and God demands it, too. It's good and acceptable in the sight of God our Savior that a believer prays – praying for all men and the people in authority.

God answers prayers. Believers should learn to go to God with full assurance and confidence that He answers prayers.

The Scriptures show it too, that God commands that we pray. As the Bible directs, believers are to pray without ceasing (1 Thess. 5:17).

A minister of the gospel once said, that prayer is both a privilege and a duty. I agree, but I hasten to add that it's more of duty.

Thank God for the wonderful privilege of prayer. But if you fail to exercise the duty or responsibility called prayer, it loses its significance and beauty, and will avail nothing (no results). Exercising the duty of prayer avails much in terms of miracles and breakthroughs. The Scripture says the fervent prayer of the righteous produces great results (Jas. 5:16).

Wonders of Prayer

The great things we desire and hope for cannot come except on the wings of prayer. Check out the history, the great moves of God in various generations have happened only in answer to prayers. An example is the great healing revival in America in early twentieth century.

Prayer is a wonder-activator. God will do no great things except men pray. That's why He commands us to ask that we may receive (Matt. 7:7-8).

Another example is when Peter was arrested, after James was murdered by Herod. It was the fervent prayer of believers that brought the manifestation of the power of God upon the prison, and Peter became a free man (Acts 5).

As a believer, do you desire to see the glory of God in your life? Pray and praise without ceasing.

King David had great testimonies of divine intervention because he was a praise addict. And he vowed his praise to God in the following psalms.

Ps. 34:1-3

> **I will bless the Lord at all times; His praise shall continually be in my mouth.**
>
> **2 My soul shall make its boast in the Lord; the humble shall hear of it and be glad.**
>
> **3 Oh, magnify the Lord with me, and let us exalt His name together.**

Praise is another great miracle-activator. Most of the wonders prayers could not deliver, came through with praise. With praise, is divine presence, glory, deliverance, miracles and victory.

King Jehoshaphat of old won a great battle with praise (2 Chron. 20). Paul and Silas 'broke' out of Philippi jail with praise. Whatever deliverance, miracle or breakthrough prayer could not deliver, praise does quite well.

Men ought to pray. But more importantly, a believer ought to be, not just a person of prayer but also of praise; a great worshipper – a praise-addict. Hallelujah!

Get addicted to praise, and you will see the glory of God in your life.

How to Pray

The best prayers – result oriented prayer – are those that are wound around the Word of God. The Bible contains great and diverse promises of God on virtually all life issues. Anchor your prayers on these promises. Build your prayer life around the Word of God, because the Word of God cannot fail, and it has never failed.

2 Peter 1:3-4 says God has given to believers all things that pertain to life, and these great gifts are situated in His Word.

When you put God to remembrance concerning His promises (His Word), you get results. It's so because, God treasures His Word above all His name, and He does not lie (Ps. 138:2; Num. 23:19).

Moreover, pray in faith and with faith. Put doubt and unbelief away; put anxiety and worry to the burner (Phil. 4:6). Ask, believing that you do have God's answers.

In the gospel of Mark chapter eleven, Jesus made one of the greatest statements about prayer.

Mark 11:23-24

> **23 For assuredly, I say to you, whoever says to this mountain, 'Be removed and be cast into the sea,' and does not doubt in his heart, but believes that those things he says will be done, he will have whatever he says.**
>
> **24 Therefore I say to you, whatever things you ask when you pray, believe that you receive them, and you will have them.**

There's a tripod upon which result-oriented prayer sits – the Word, Faith and the Name of Jesus Christ.

That's also why Jesus said, whatever you ask the Father in His name, shall be granted to you (John 16:23-24).

Believers ought to walk by faith and not by sight (2 Cor. 5:7). The prayer that pleases God is that anchored on the Word of God with faith in the name of Jesus.

When you go to God with His Word on the golden plate of faith, you cannot fail – you will certainly succeed and achieve your desires. We have this confidence in God, that when we ask anything according to His will, we get an answer (1 John 5:14-15).

I say again, pray and praise without ceasing. Hallelujah!

Printed in the United States
By Bookmasters